Legal Almanac Series No. 40

THE BILL OF RIGHTS AND THE POLICE

By MELVYN ZARR

This Legal Almanac has been revised by the Oceana Editorial Staff

Irving J. Sloan
General Editor

SECOND EDITION

1980 Oceana Publications, Inc.
Dobbs Ferry, New York 10522

This is a newly revised edition of the fortieth number in a series of LEGAL ALMANACS which bring you the law on various subjects in nontechnical language. These books do not take the place of your attorney's advice, but they can introduce you to your legal rights and responsibilities.

Library of Congress Cataloging in Publication Data

Zarr, Melvyn, 1936-
    The Bill of Rights and the police.

    (Legal almanac series; 40)
    Includes index.
    1.   Criminal procedure--United States--Popular works.
2.   Police--United States--Popular works.   I. Title.
KF9625.Z9Z3   1980   345.73'052   79-28179
ISBN 0-379-11130-6

52273

81-13942

345.73
ZAR

TABLE OF CONTENTS

FOREWORD

The thrust of this small book has been to convey the idea that the guarantees of the Bill of Rights are neither technicalities nor rigid, inflexible rules; that they incorporate fundamental principles basic to the preservation of a decent society, free from the procedures of a police state; and that they are not at war with common sense or the needs of order and security.

The liberties of a people are seldom lost to frontal attack; usually they are destroyed under the guise of attacking a grave national problem. Thus, easy "law and order" solutions destructive of individual liberty must be resisted, for two reasons: 1) it has not been demonstrated that our crime problem is causally related to enforcement of the protections of the Bill of Rights; and 2) even were this so, would not the methods of a police state be too high a price to pay?

The principles incorporated in the Bill of Rights are continually being adjusted to the changing conditions of our society. That task is a delicate and sensitive one, and is ultimately committed to the Supreme Court of the United States. But all of us must be involved in the process. The laws and procedures which test the quality of our civilization must not only be fair and efficient, but they must be appreciated by the citizenry to be so. Local policemen, local prosecutors, local judges and local citizens generally must all understand and respect the protections of the Bill of Rights. Otherwise, they will be only so many platitudes, useless except for filling up academic tracts.

Toward this goal of public understanding and respect, this book is dedicated.

Chapter 1:

THE LIBERTY vs. SECURITY BALANCING ACT

There is a real tension in our society between the need for more effective police work to combat the rising tide of crime and our constitutional aversion to a police state. This is a central fact which no amount of simplistic sloganeering can erase. This tension cannot be avoided simply by calling for "law and order," or more aggressive police tactics. This tension is part and parcel of every civilized society; each is obliged to strike its own balance between security and liberty—even one that discharges that function covertly and resolves most issues in favor of public order and security.

Our Bill of Rights—our balance—was struck in reaction to the balance struck in 18th Century England. That society opted for order and security by, among other things, punishing hundreds of crimes by death and by empowering its constabulary to search and seize at will under the authority of general warrants.

To the Framers of our Constitution, liberty was poorly weighted in that balance. They recognized the tendency of even well-meaning officials, once caught up in the excitement of pursuit of suspected criminals, to use whatever short-cut seemed most effective and to ignore the liberties of the citizenry. The police cure, they thought, could often be worse than the social ill.

Accordingly, the Framers built into our Constitution principles to protect the liberties of United States citizens. These devices were hammered out after hard debate and compromise. They were devised as restraints on official action. They were frankly acknowledged not to make crime fighting any easier; other interests in addition to police efficiency were sought to be protected. Accordingly, a Bill of Rights was framed which embodies a profound national commitment to keep the police within our control.

But the Bill of Rights was not seen as a set of rigid rules to make the task of maintaing order and security unnecessarily harder. The Framers were not insensible to the real need of the citizenry for protection. They recognized that a society unable to protect its citizens encourages each citizen to become his own policeman and fosters a system of private justice. Moreover, a Bill of Rights artificially and unnecessarily obstructive of citizen protection would not command enough respect to be enforced.

Therefore, the Bill of Rights struck a balance which protected fundamental incidents of liberty, while at the same time protecting public order and the citizen's security. The Bill of Rights imposes limits on the power of a policeman to stop a person from speaking or picketing, or arrest his freedom of movement, or search his person or home, or subject him to questioning. That the effect of these limitations may be to restrain policemen in their pursuit of suspected criminals cannot justify their abandonment. In our society, the Bill of Rights settled that.

Let us consider a case in constitutional adjudication. In a small city, a woman called the police and claimed that she has been raped. She could not identify her attacker beyond the general description that he was a Negro youth. The police dusted the window of entry for fingerprints and found some. Guided only by this general description and the set of fingerprints, the police decided to round up all the Negro youths in the area for fingerprinting and questioning. As it turned out, one of the 70 Negro youths rounded up furnished prints which matched those on the victim's window. The boy was convicted. Good police work? A triumph for "law and order"? No, held the United States Supreme Court, condemning the police conduct in the case. Why? The decision would be unexplainable were the sole object of our society for the police to get their man. But this premise is incorrect: our Bill of Rights, specifically the Fourth Amendment, forbids dragnet arrests of the kind just described. It forbids the police to ignore the rights of the dozens of innocent youths picked up in the dragnet. It protects against this by requiring the police to get a warrant for an arrest, which can only be obtained by demonstrating to a judge that there is probable cause to believe that a particular person is guilty of the crime.[1]

In the case just described, the Supreme Court construed the Fourth Amendment's proscription of "unreasonable searches and seizures." Other provisions of the Bill of Rights impinging upon police conduct are equally general. The First Amendment protects "freedom of speech, or of the press; or the right of the people peaceably to assemble, and to petition the Government for a redress of grievances." The Fifth Amendment restrains the police from " compelling " any person to incriminate himself.

These general principles are constantly being applied to new fact situations and adjusted with new conceptions of, and challenges to, our society. At any given time there are always more constitutional questions left open than settled. The responsibility for this process of application and adjustment falls ultimately on the Justices of the United States Supreme Court. Theirs is the most difficult balancing act in our society.

This book will attempt to outline where the balance has been struck in the crucial issues of police power and individual liberty. Constitutional doctrine is never static, and sometimes the rate of change is dizzingly fast. But the closing of the Warren era of the Court gives us an opportunity to assess the situation at a time when future rapid constitutional change seems unlikely.

In the following chapters we shall treat the constitutional limitations on the police power to inhibit free speech activities, to define criminal conduct under vaguely worded criminal laws, to stop or arrest persons, to search persons, homes or businesses, and to interrogate and otherwise investigate persons taken into custody.

---

[1] *Davis v. Mississippi,* 394 U.S. 721 (1969).

3

A caveat must be repeated: the constitutional balance described herein is not graven in stone, but only printed on the pages of the Supreme Court's decisions. These decisions are readable, and should be read, for each generation of citizens and lawyers must take part in keeping the balance true.

Chapter 2

POLICE INTERFERENCE AND
FIRST AMENDMENT RIGHTS

The First Amendment

. . . or abridging the freedom of speech, or of the press; or of right of the people peaceably to assemble, and to petition the government for a redress of grievances.

The First Amendment differs in a very important way from other provisions of the Bill of Rights . . . which restrict police action. These other provisions deal with police procedures: procedures which the police must follow in conducting arrests, searches, and interrogations and other investigative measures. They require, under certain circumstances, a warrant for an arrest or search, certain warnings to be given prior to custodial interrogation, and provision of counsel. And although the Fourth Amendment, as construed, requires in general terms that a policeman not interfere with a citizen unless he has a certain quantum of evidence of crime, it does not direct the policeman to let alone certain citizen conduct.

The First Amendment, on the other hand, is specifically and uniquely directed to insulating certain kinds of conduct from police interference. Because it is generally phrased and offers wide opportunity for interpretation, interpretation has not been static. Indeed, it was not until this century that the Supreme Court recognized that the First Amendment delimits the power of state as well as federal officials.

What freedom is encompassed within "freedom of speech"? What are the limits on the "right of the people peaceably to assemble"? These are some of the questions which have troubled and divided the Supreme Court. It is possible, but not very helpful, to recite various statements taken from Supreme Court opinions as the "law" of the First Amendment. But bare statements do not decide real cases. One must examine where the balance between freedom and order has been struck in the context of real fact situations coming before the Court.

There are many forms of communication which fall under the general protection of "freedom of speech." They may be regulated in different ways according to their nature and function. The kinds of restrictions which the First Amendment permits to be imposed upon communication fall, generally, into three categories. The individual's interest in communication must be adjusted with the governmental interest in: (1) protecting the rights of others not to listen if they so choose; (2) protecting others from injurious consequences of the communication; and (3) protecting some governmental function.

An illustration of the first category is where the speaker physically restrains his audience in order to make it listen. Whether this involves preventing a college dean from leaving or entering his office in order to make him pay attention or interrupting a church service in order to preach the disrupters' brand of religion, the First Amendment does not insulte this form of communication. The rights of others not to listen must be respected. Thus, for example, the Supreme Court has allowed state prohibitions on the use of sound trucks in residential neighborhoods.

An illustration of the second category is provided by Justice Holmes' famous dictum that the First Amendment does not protect one who falsely shouts "fire" in a crowded theater. Likewise, speech which incites to riot, furthers a conspiracy to commit crimes, invades the privacy of others or maliciously libels another is not protected by the First Amendment. For example, the First Amendment insulates false charges against government officials on the theory "that debate on public issues should be uninhibited, robust and wide-open, and . . . may well include vehement, caustic and sometimes unpleasantly sharp attacks on government and public officials." But there is a limit. The Supreme Court has held that this protection does not run to false statements about public officials made with actual malice against them.

A third justification for regulating or prohibiting some kinds of communications is to protect some governmental function. Communication in the form of plotting a revolution, arranging a political assassination or communicating intelligence to the enemy is not protected.

Let us consider *Street v. New York*, 394 U.S. 576 (1969). On June 6, 1966, Sidney Street was sitting in his Brooklyn apartment listening to the radio. He heard a news report that civil rights leader James Meredith had been shot by a sniper in Mississippi. Muttering to himself, "They didn't protect him," Street, himself a Negro, took from his drawer a neatly folded 48-Star American flag, which he formerly had displayed on national holidays, and carried the still-folded flag to a nearby street corner. There, he lit the flag with a match, and dropped it on the pavement when it began to burn. A small crowd began to gather and an approaching policeman heard Street say, "We don't need no damn flag." When the policeman asked Street whether he had burned the flag he replied, "Yes; that is my flag; I burned it. If they let that happen to Meredith, we don't need an American flag." Street was charged not only with burning the flag, but also with casting contempt upon it by his words. He was convicted on both charges. In April, 1969, the Supreme Court reversed his conviction for making derogatory remarks about the flag, on the ground that they were encompassed within the "freedom of speech" protection of the First Amendment, in the absence of any substantial governmental interest in punishing the speech.

The Supreme Court examined four governmental interests which might conceivably have been furthered by punishing Street for his words. First, there might have been an interest in deterring Street from vocally inciting others to commit unlawful acts. But Street's words, taken alone, did not urge anyone to do anything unlawful. They amounted to somewhat excited public advocacy of the idea that the United States should abandon, at least temporarily, one of its national symbols. Such public advocacy of peaceful change in our institutions, the Supreme Court held, is protected by the First Amendment (as made applicable to the States by the due process clause of the Fourteenth Amendment).

Second, there might have been a governmental interest in preventing Street from uttering words so inflamatory that they would provoke others to retaliate physically against him, thereby causing a breach of the peace. The Supreme Court rejected this rationale on the ground that Street's remarks were not so inherently inflamatory as to come within that small class of "fighting words" which are likely to provoke the average person to retaliation, and thereby cause a breach of the peace.

Third, there might have been a governmental interest in protecting the sensibilities of passers-by who might have been shocked by Street's words about the American flag. The Supreme Court rejected this theory on the ground that any shock effect must be attributed to the content of the ideas expressed and held: "It is firmly settled that under our Constitution the public expression of ideas may not be prohibited merely because the ideas are themselves offensive to some of their hearers."

Fourth and finally, there might have been a governmental interest in assuring that Street show proper respect for our national emblem. Stating that "disrespect for our flag is to be deplored no less in these vexed times than in calmer periods of our history," the Supreme Court nevertheless relied upon an earlier case, decided during World War II, to reject this theory of conviction. In a case striking down a public school regulation requiring unwilling schoolchildren to salute the flag, the Court had held:

> Freedom to differ is not limited to things that do
> not matter much. That would be a mere shadow of
> freedom. The test of its substance is the right to differ
> as to things that touch the heart of the existing order.
> If there is any fixed star in our constitutional con-
> stellation, it is that no official, high or petty, can
> prescribe what shall be orthodox in politics, na-
> tionalism, religion, or other matters of opinion, or
> force citizens to confess by word or act their faith
> therein.

The Court did not need to reach the question whether the First Amendment protected the symbolic act of burning the flag.

But the Court has answered the question whether the First Amendment protects the burning of draft cards. On March 31, 1966, David Paul O'Brien and three of his companions burned their draft cards on the steps of the South Boston Courthouse. A sizable crowd, including several FBI agents, witnessed the event. O'Brien stated to the agents that he had burned his draft card publicly in order to influence others to adopt his anti-war beliefs. In the Supreme Court, he took the position that his burning of the draft card was a form of symbolic speech which communicated his opposition to the war and the draft. O'Brien was not prosecuted for failing to have his draft card in his possession; rather, he was prosecuted under a 1965 Act of Congress which made it a crime to intentionally destroy one's draft card. O'Brien contended that, since failure to possess the draft card was already a criminal offense, the purpose and effect of the 1965 act under which he was prosecuted could only be to punish the dissent expressed by the act of burning a draft card. The United States Court of Appeals for the First Circuit agreed with this argument and declared the act unconstitutional.

However, in an 8-1 decision of the Supreme Court authored by Chief Justice Warren, the Supreme Court upheld the act. The Court began by recognizing that there was an element of communication in the draft card burning, but held that the punishment of this communication was "incidental" to the punishment of the burning, which the government had a sufficiently important interest in prohibiting. This important interest in deterring men from burning their draft cards was declared to be: "The smooth and proper functioning of the system that Congress has established to raise armies."[2]

Nevertheless, the Court left open several possibilities that might compel a different result. First, if Congress were to legislate against "incidental" speech by measures which did not seek to enforce its interest in the narrowest possible way, then such an act might be unconstitutional. Second, if Congress had passed an act specifically aimed at suppressing communication,

---

[2] *United States v. O'Brien*, 391 U.S. 367 (1968).

9

"it could not be sustained as a regulation of noncommunicative conduct." Third, Justice Harlan, in a concurring opinion, stated that a different result might have been reached if O'Brien had had no other means at his disposal—other than burning his draft card—to protest the war and the draft.

Permissible governmental restrictions and regulations of incidents of peaceable assembly like picketing, parading and other protest demonstrations parallel those of free speech.

The classic statement of the general principle of peaceable assembly was stated 30 years ago in a Supreme Court opinion:

> Wherever the title of streets and parks may rest, they
> have immemorially been held in trust for the use of
> the public and, time out of mind, have been used for
> purposes of assembling, communicating thoughts
> between citizens, and discussing public questions.
> Such use of the streets and public places has, from
> ancient times, been a part of the privileges, im-
> munities, rights and liberties of citizens.

But this right, as others, is not absolute and may be regulated. The permissible theories of regulation may again be divided into three categories. First, demonstrators may not force anyone to pay attention to their demonstration.

Second, demonstrators must respect the rights of others to be free from unwarranted consequences of them. Demonstrators may not block others' entry or exit from buildings and may not block vehicular or pedestrian traffic upon the streets or sidewalks. Although peaceful demonstrations carried on in locations open to the public may not be absolutely prohibited, they may be subject to regulation. The nature of this regulation was analyzed in an opinion by the Supreme Court in 1965, which reviewed a great many of the free speech and peaceable assembly cases and summarized them in this way:

> From these decisions certain clear principles emerge.
> The rights of free speech and assembly, while fun-
> damental in our democratic society, still do not mean
> that everyone with opinions and beliefs may address

a group at any public place and at any time. The constitutional guarantee of liberty implies the existence of an organized society maintaining public order, without which liberty itself would be lost in the excesses of anarchy. The control of travel on the streets is a clear example of governmental responsibility to ensure this necessary order. . . . One would not be justified in ignoring the familiar red light because this was thought to be a means of social protest. Nor could one, contrary to traffic regulations, insist upon a street meeting in the middle of Times Square at the rush hour as a form of freedom of speech or assembly. Governmental authorities have the duty and responsibility to keep their streets open and available for movement. A group of demonstrators could not insist upon the right to cordon off a street, or entrance to a public or private building, and allow no one to pass who did not agree to listen to their exhortations. . . .

Third, states may impose an absolute ban on demonstrations in certain areas reserved for governmental operations which would be interrupted by such demonstrations. In 1966, the Supreme Court held that the state of Florida could validly prohibit and punish any demonstrations in a jail house yard, on the ground that such demonstrations would interfere with the orderly operation of the jail.

One form of regulation is that exemplified by laws requiring permits for parades. In 1963, Rev. Martin Luther King, Jr. and over 1,000 others were arrested in Birmingham for parading without a permit. The Supreme Court, in 1969, threw out these convictions on the ground that the permit-issuing authorities had too much discretion to grant or refuse a permit, in that a city ordinance authorized them to deny a permit if, in their judgment, the public "welfare," "decency," or "morals" required it. These standards were held to be too vague and susceptible to abuse to be constitutional.

Vagueness is similarly prohibited in other kinds of penal

11

laws. Offenses such as breach of the peace or disorderly conduct sweep in a great variety of conduct under a vague and overly broad definition and leave to the executive and judicial branches too wide a discretion in their application.

An example is given by a civil rights case decided by the Supreme Court in 1963. About 200 Negro high school and college students left a church in Columbia, South Carolina and marched toward the State Capitol. They walked in groups of about 15, in such a way as not to obstruct pedestrian or vehicular traffic. When they arrived at the Capitol grounds, they gathered in a horseshoe area of the grounds open to the public. There they heard speeches, and sang and clapped their hands. After about 15 minutes they were all arrested and charged with breach of the peace. The Supreme Court reversed these convictions, holding:

> We do not review in this case criminal convictions resulting from the evenhanded application of a precise and narrowly drawn regulatory statute evincing a legislative judgment that certain specific conduct be limited or proscribed.

> If, for example, the petitioners had been convicted upon evidence that they had violated a law regulating traffic, or had disobeyed a law reasonably limiting the periods during which the State House grounds were open to the public, this would be a different case.

The Supreme Court held that the offense of breach of the ·peace was so vague and indefinite as to allow persons to be convicted for peaceably expressing unpopular views.[3]

In the next chapter we shall deal further with the vitally important requirement that criminal laws be definite and specific and give the policeman only narrowly circumsribed discretion. We shall see that this vagueness doctrine is important not only in the enforcement of First Amendment rights, but in the much broader context of the general right of all citizens to be let alone by the police.

---

[3] *Edwards v. South Carolina,* 372 U.S. 229 (1963).

Chapter 3

POLICE POWERS AND
CONSTITUTIONAL PROTECTION

The Bill of Rights, as it impinges upon police action, deals not with what conduct should be let alone but with how police interference with that conduct shall be carried out. It deals with procedures:

1. What procedures must a policeman follow in seizing a person, i.e., depriving him of his freedom of movement? (This Chapter);

2. What procedures must a policeman follow in searching a person? (Chapter 8); and,

3. What procedures must a policeman follow in interrogating a person or otherwise investigating him? (Chapter 7).

The problem of providing remedies for police breaches of any of these duties, including the duty to refrain from excessive force in performing police functions, is treated in Chapter 7.

What procedure must police follow in effecting a seizure of a person? The general rule is that he must have a warrant. This follows from the Warrant Clause of the Fourth Amendment: "No warrants shall issue, but upon probable cause, supported by oath or affirmation, and particularly describing the place to be searched, and the persons or things to be seized."

The rationale of the warrant requirement is not to further burden the police with more paperwork, but to keep sensi-

13

tive judgments about a citizen's liberty out of police hands and in the hands of impartial, detached judicial officers, where they belong. As the Supreme Court made clear many years ago: "The point of the Fourth Amendment, which often is not grasped by zealous officers, is not that it denies law enforcement the support of the usual inferences which reasonable men draw from evidence. Its protection consists in requiring that those inferences be drawn by a neutral and detached magistrate instead of being judged by the officer engaged in the often competitive enterprise of ferreting out crime."

The efficacy of the warrant rule can only be gauged by its performance in the crucible of the streets. In the streets, where the tension between order and liberty is greatest, the police are daily confronted with manifold challenges to adjust the need to protect citizens from street crimes, such as mugging, with the need to maintain free passage for everyone—whether they be potential muggers or potential victims. But it is there that the warrant rule is daily diluted or ignored.

In the streets, a warrant is the last thing a policeman has or thinks he needs. The police can arrest without a warrant if they have probable cause to believe that the citizen they are confronting has committed a serious crime (a felony). Probable cause is defined to exist where the facts and surrounding circumstances of which the arresting officer has reasonably trustworthy information would justify a man of reasonable caution in believing that a crime has been committed by the person to be arrested. Generally speaking, police can also seize a person without a warrant if he is committing a less serious crime (a misdemeanor) in their presence. These exceptions do much to swallow up the warrant rule. After all, a policeman can almost always justify a seizure of a person by stating that he caught that person in the act of committing the misdemeanor of loitering or being a vagrant in his presence. Laws such as vagrancy or loitering, in conjunction with the power of police to arrest without a warrant for misdemeanors committed in their presence, do much to erode the warrant requirement. These loose laws are used as street-cleaning devices to keep citizens "in line" on the streets or to run them in. Whether or not the

14

criminal charges are dismissed or lead to conviction is of marginal importance: the important thing is that "undesirables" are kept moving or taken off the streets. Arrest now is worth a hundred times conviction later.

Further erosion of the warrant requirement—and of the protections surrounding arrest without a warrant—was provided by the Supreme Court in 1968, in upholding police power to "stop and frisk." The facts of the case were these. On Euclid Avenue in Cleveland, on a fall afternoon in 1963, a plainclothesman detective observed two men standing on a street corner. For some reason which he could not articulate, they attracted his attention. He observed one man leave the corner, walk past a store window, stop, continue on, turn around, return to the second man and confer with him on the street corner. After this, the second man went through the same series of motions and returned to the street corner to confer with his companion. Each did this five or six times. The plainclothesman decided: "They don't look right to me." He then observed as the two men continued on a few blocks and met a third. At that point the plainclothesman confronted them and asked for their names. When the men "mumbled something," the plainclothesman responded by grabbing one, spinning him around to face the other two and patting down the outside of his clothing. The plainclothesman felt something hard, removed the man's overcoat and found a gun. He then arrested the man for illegal possession of a weapon. The plainclothesman had no warrant to arrest the man nor, prior to the time he grabbed him, did he have probable cause to believe that the man had committed or was committing a felony. The Supreme Court held (8-1) that this constituted necessary and proper police work because the plainclothesman had enough "reasonable suspicion" that the men were up to no good to grab one man, spin him around, pat down his clothing and remove and search his overcoat.[4]

The net effect of this decision is that if you are stopped on the street by a policeman and asked your name, or anything

---

[4] This case is *Terry v. Ohio,* 392 U.S. 1 (1968).

15

else, you had better not mumble. Instead, you had better speak up and give answers that satisfy the policeman. Otherwise your stop may continue, you may be frisked, or you may be arrested for, say loitering. What *will* satisfy the policeman is not clear. That depends a good deal on the policeman.

Another aspect of warrantless arrests involving the plights of two New York City men, one arrested for murder, the other for illegal drug possession is before the United States Supreme Court at the time of publishing this volume in a crucial test of a policeman's right to enter a home to make an arrest without a warrant in a nonemergency situation.

When the Supreme Court rules in this case late in 1979, its decision may well be the long-awaited definitive ruling on the issue of arrests without warrants.

As in all these situations, at the center of the dispute is the sanctity of a person's home versus the need of law enforcement officers to apprehend a criminal suspect. Generally, prosecutors and other law enforcement officers assert that arrest warrants are not needed when the police have "probable cause," or good reason, to believe that a person has committed a crime. Defense attorneys, while not disputing a policeman's right to make a warrantless arrest in an emergency situation, argue that the greater protection of a warrant must be afforded a suspect when no emergency exists and when the suspect himself, rather than his possessions, is sought by the police.

The New York State Court of Appeals, that State's highest Court, upheld the right of the police to arrest the men. In each case, the police without obtaining a warrant entered the defendant's apartment to make an arrest and found evidence that was used at the trial. The State Court upheld the arrests, seizure of evidence and convictions. It ruled, 4 to 3, that warrant requirements for arrests could be less strict than those for searches because of the "substantial difference between the intrusion that attends entry for the purpose of searching the premises and that which results from an entry for the purpose of making an arrest." The Court noted that entry for search involved "rummaging through possessions" and discovering "personal items and details" that a person would "expect to be free from scrutiny from uninvited eyes."

In an entry for arrest, however, the New York decision found that there is "no accompanying prying into the area of expected privacy."

Again, the courts have long upheld the right of the police to make searches of a criminal suspect's immediate vicinity when he is arrested. The police did so in the cases of these defendants, one who was convicted in the death of a service station attendant, and the other who was convicted of criminal possession of a controlled substance.

In each case, evidence discovered in the defendant's home was used at the trial. The defendants contend that the evidence should have been suppressed because it was seized in nonemergency situations by police officers who did not have arrest warrants.

Although the United States Supreme Court has said that the issue of warrantless arrests was "still unsettled," particularly when an arrest is made in a suspect's home, it has made decisions that have skirted the issues raised in these cases.

In 1976 the High Court ruled, 5 to 3, that a law enforcement officer may make an arrest without a warrant in a public place even if there had been adequate opportunity to obtain a warrant. All the Constitution requires, said the Court, is that the police have probable cause to believe that the person being arrested has committed a felony. In the same year, in another case, the Court ruled, 7 to 2, that when the police have probable cause to make an arrest and they see a suspect in the doorway of his home, they may pursue him into the house even if they do not have an arrest warrant.

The fact is that the courts have almost always held that police officers do not need warrants in emergencies, such as when they are in hot pursuit of a suspect, when they believe that evidence may be destroyed or when a suspect is likely to flee. But when no emergency exists, innocent people should be protected. People's homes are important and privileged places, and this is what the Fourth Amendment protects. After all, police are required to obtain warrants for wiretaps and such minimal purposes as searches of footlockers. Surely, then, a suspect should receive greater protection when the police grab his person and take him to the precinct.

How the Supreme Court will rule in any case is rarely certain, but the present Burger Court has shown a tendency in recent years to take a sterner stance toward defendant's assertions of Fourth Amendment rights than did the Warren Court. The Civil Liberties Union, however, has optimistically predicted that the Court will rule in favor of the defendants in these New York cases. It observes that the Supreme Court has been very careful about creating exceptions to warrant requirements.

Arrest today is a "doomsday" device. Police records and computers indelibly put the "mark of Cain" on any citizen who is arrested. His or her criminal record will pursue him or her all the days of their lives. Educational and employment opportunities narrow drastically for anyone who has been arrested in this country and with our frontier now gone, the person with a record has nowhere to go but down.

Police arrest powers, then, in modern America are indeed awesome powers. These police arrest powers have both the power to protect society and the power to destroy the citizen. The Fourth Amendment was designed to limit the chances of a citizen being destroyed- unfairly or unjustly. The courts have the responsibility to make sure the Fourth Amendment works to protect the citizen and, at the same time, assure the security of society.

Chapter 4

SEARCH AND SEIZURE PROCEDURES
AND THE FOURTH AMENDMENT

The Fourth Amendment

The right of the people to be secure in their person, houses, papers, and effects, against unreasonable searches and seizures, shall not be violated, and no warrants shall issue, but upon probable cause, supported by oath or affirmation, and particularly describing the place to be searched, and the persons or things to be seized.

Here, as in the previous chapter, we start with a general protective rule and examine its limitations in practice. The general rule, as recently stated by the Supreme Court, is as follows:

> One governing principle, justified by history and by current experience, has consistently been followed: except in certain carefully defined classes of cases, a search of private property without proper consent is 'unreasonable' unless it has been authorized by a valid search warrant.

Thus, as a general rule, a search warrant is required if a policeman wishes to search you, your home, car or business. The warrant is not a trifling technicality, but evidences the fact that a neutral, detached magistrate, and not simply a policeman, has determined that the search should be made. The warrant requirement was written into the Bill of Rights because of the experience of the Colonies with general warrants, which allowed police officers to roam at will, wherever they chose, in search of persons or contraband. Clearly and repeatedly, the Supreme Court has stated its insistence that the high function of the search warrant be respected:

> We are not dealing with formalities. The presence of a search warrant serves a high function. Absent some grave emergency, the Fourth Amendment has

19

interposed a magistrate between the citizen and the police. This was done not to shield criminals nor to make the home a safe haven for illegal activities. It was done so that an objective mind might weigh the need to invade that privacy in order to enforce the law. The right of privacy was deemed too precious to entrust to the discretion of those whose job is the detection of crime and the arrest of criminals. . . . And so the Constitution requires a magistrate to pass on the desires of the police before they violate the privacy of the home. We cannot be true to that constitutional requirement and excuse the absence of a search warrant without a showing by those who seek exemption from the constitutional mandate that the exigencies of the situation make that course imperative.

Of course, the general rule is no stronger than the weakest of its exceptions, and in this area they are many.

First of all, the warrant requirement is excused altogether when there are "exigent circumstances" making the securing of a warrant impracticable. Thus in the case of a moving vehicle, which can be quickly driven out of the locality or jurisdiction in which the warrant must be sought, a warrantless search can be conducted.

A second exception is permitted when consent is given by the individual whose person or premises is to be searched. To be valid, such consent must be freely given, and based upon the assurance that the police will not search anyway if consent is withheld.

A third occasion for warrantless search is permitted when police are making a lawful arrest. In this case, the police may search without a warrant the area from which the person being arrested might gain possession of a weapon or destructible evidence. Pursuant to such a lawful arrest, the police may also take fingerprints and statements, although as to the latter, there are additional requirements upon police deriving from the Fifth Amendment's privilege against self-incrimination, which we shall treat in the next chapter.

Not only may a search warrant be entirely excused, but justification for its issuance may be somewhat relaxed.

Thus, search warrants for businesses may be obtained by health and building code inspectors upon a non-individualized showing of probable cause. In other words, a business may be searched for one administrative reason or another when the inspector has no particular reason to believe that it fails to meet administrative standards, but simply because its area is ripe for inspection.

Another case in which the Supreme Court has hinted that the requirement of probable cause may be relaxed is that of a warrant for taking a person into custody for the limited purpose of fingerprinting him. What this lessened standard of probable cause might be remains to be explicated by the Supreme Court.

A special problem is presented when police wish to search a home—not pursuant to an arrest—but in order to effect a lawful arrest pursuant to an arrest warrant. In such a case, the necessity of a search warrant is an open question, although a good case can be made for requiring one. The functions of search warrants and arrest warrants are materially different. The arrest warrant evidences a judicial determination that there is probable cause to believe a person guilty of crime. The search warrant evidences a judicial determination that there is probable cause to believe that the persons or things to be seized are within the premises to be searched. Thus an officer in possession of an arrest warrant would appear to have no judicial authorization to search premises other than those of the person to be seized. Of course, if the suspect is actually seen entering the premises, and it is reasonably feared that he will not stay there long enough to enable the police to get a search warrant, then, of course, "exigent circumstances" necessary to excuse the warrant might be presented. On the other hand, to permit the police to search homes or other premises merely on the suspicion that the person for whom they have an arrest warrant might be present would be to elevate the arrest warrant to the status of a general search warrant—against which the

Fourth Amendment was specifically directed. Nevertheless, as previously indicated, the courts have yet to come to grips with this problem.

Another problem awaiting resolution lies in the area of searches of college dormitories. It is true that the college, rather than the student, owns the dormitory. But does this entitle college officials to search or authorize police to search these rooms without a warrant? College authorities have assumed this power, but whether that assumption of power is constitutional remains to be seen. Recently the Supreme Court held that a man using a public telephone booth was entitled to the protections of the Fourth Amendment. That amendment, the Supreme Court explained, protects people, not places, and protects them wherever they have the reasonable expectation of privacy.

Yet another unresolved problem is that presented by government assertions of power as to wiretapping and bugging. These methods have been held to be "searches" for purposes of the Fourth Amendment. The open question is whether warrants authorizing wiretapping and bugging meet the Fourth Amendment requirement of "particularly describing . . . the persons or things to be seized." The things being "seized" by wiretaps and other electronic surveillance devices are, of course, conversations. The means employed are obviously pervasive and nonselective. Thus, a wiretap or bug picks up *all* conversations, not just those in which the eavesdropper has a predetermined interest. In 1967, the Supreme Court invalidated a New York statute on the ground that the warrant authorized thereunder did not " particularly describe " the conversations to be seized. The following year, the Congress passed a federal statute explicitly attempting to plug the constitutional gaps found in the New York statute and authorizing wiretapping and bugging on a national scale. Whether this effort will pass constitutional muster is an open question, which may depend just as much on the changes on the Court as on the differences in the statutes.

Most recently, the Government has asserted a power to conduct wiretapping and bugging *without* a warrant in "national security" or "internal security" cases. The asserted justification for excusing the statute's warrant requirement is that judges cannot be expected to appreciate the foreign policy needs of the country and that the necessity for wiretaps and bugs of, say, foreign embassies is best left to the discretion of the President or Attorney General. Whatever the merits of this contention, the Government is now seeking to apply it to persons or organizations which the Attorney General deems inimical to the eternal security of the country, as, for example, those persons under federal indictment for leading and participating in demonstrations at the Democratic National Convention in Chicago in August, 1968. (That case also provides an example of the use of vaguely worded laws to overreach conduct which may fall within the First Amendment area.)

A recent development in the law of search warrants to search innocent *third* parties is worth noting at this point. In 1978, the Supreme Court held in the California case of *Zurcher v. Stanford Daily,* that unannounced searches of innocent third parties are constitutional. The Santa Clara County District Attorney had sent his deputies on a surprise raid of the offices of the college newspaper offices of the *Stanford Daily.* They were looking for unpublished pictures of a demonstration which, the D.A. believed, would enable him to identify certain student assailants of certain bruised policemen.

The police did not find what they were after but they did poke through filing cabinets, desk drawers, shelves, wastebaskets, and private notes and correspondence including names of some of the reporters' confidential sources.

No one claimed that anyone on the *Stanford Daily* staff was suspected of a crime. They were innocent third parties. And, for the first time, the courts through the *Zurcher* case, were going to determine whether police, on the basis of a search warrant, could legally conduct a surprise raid on the offices or homes of third parties who themselves are not under suspicion.

There was no record of any previous state or Federal court decision that such a search is harmful. It had always been assumed that if you were a law-abiding citizen the least the

23

police could do—if they thought you might have evidence they were looking for—was to give you some notice, not just barge in the door like they do where the Free Worlds ends. After all, prosecutors and police officers who are not just fishing can get a subpoena, a judge will decide if they have a right to search.

In arguing before the Supreme Court that the unannounced search of the *Stanford Daily* had been unconstitutional, the paper's lawyers had two main lines of attack. These police swoops were exactly what the Framers of the Constitution wanted to bar when they guaranteed "the right of the people to be secure in their persons, houses, papers, and effects, against unreasonable searches and seizures."

The paper's lawyers emphasized that although a newspaper is entitled to "the heightened protections of the First Amendment" in this fearsome context, *all* innocent third parties—not just press people—should be secure from surprise police raids because of the Fourth Amendment. In short, not only as readers and watchers of the news but also as citizens whose own homes and offices have been stripped of protection by the Supreme Court, are at stake in this decision.

Another consequence of this decision is the looming impact on institutional third parties. This is a reference to places where confidential information is kept on large numbers of people such as a law office, accounting firm, bank, credit bureau, private investigation firm, physician, psychiatrist, hospital, business office, etc. Under *Zurcher*, none of these institutional third parties is immune to a surprise search.

Considerable pressure is being brought to bear upon Congress to enact new laws deflecting this decision. But at this time it is the law.

Hopefully, this chapter suggests some of the ebb and flow in the law relating to searches and seizures. Here, as in other areas, there is a real tension between the professed needs of law enforcement and the liberty of the individual. The questions left unanswered are fully as important and vexing as those already settled. The protections of the Fourth Amendment, as those of the Fifth, which we shall examine in the next chapter, give indications of remaining a legal battlefield for years to come.

24

Chapter 5

POLICE PROCEDURES AND THE
CUSTODIAL INVESTIGATION

The Fifth Amendment

No person . . . shall be compelled in any criminal case to be a witness against himself . . .

The Sixth Amendment

In all criminal prosecutions, the accused shall have . . . the assistance of counsel for his defence.

Once a suspect is taken into lawful police custody to answer for a crime, to what extent can the police require his cooperation in the investigation of the crime? Here, as in other areas of police-citizen interaction, we observe a continuing tension: in this case between the need for police to obtain information of crime and the right of the citizen 1) not to be compelled to incriminate himself (provided by the Fifth Amendment) and 2) to the assistance of counsel for his defense (provided by the Sixth Amendment).

Here, as elsewhere, it is important to recognize that these rights are not mere "technicalities," enforced by hypercritical judges to needlessly handcuff the police, but are essential elements in the definition of a free society.

The Fifth Amendment's privilege against self-incrimination was framed against the background of English history, which provided grim illustration of the dangers of an inquisitorial system. Notorious in English experience was the Star Chamber proceeding, which played a sort of heads-I-win, tails-you-lose game with suspects: the witness was made either to incriminate himself or refuse to answer. In either event, he ended up on the rack and screw. Following the most notorious case in English history, involving one John Lilburn, Parliament finally recognized that the Star Chamber cure was more dangerous than the evil sought to be eradicated, and abolished it.

The Framers of the Constitution wrote the Fifth Amendment with John Lilburn in mind. They ordained an accusatorial—not an inquisitorial—system, i.e., a system whereby the prosecutor was not to rely upon wrenching guilt out of the defendant's mouth. The Framers knew, in the words of an early Supreme Court opinion, that "illegitimate and unconstitutional practices get their first footing . . . by silent approaches and slight deviations from legal modes of procedure."

In the last 30 years, this country has witnessed significant development of the privilege against self-incrimination. This development was not pre-planned and, indeed, neither it nor the controversy it has engendered could have been anticipated by the Supreme Court of 30 years ago. But, as so often happens in constitutional litigation, one small step leads to another and finally one ascends to a plateau of principle which, although altogether defensible, nonetheless offers an unexpected perspective.

In 1934, in a rural section of Mississippi, a white man was discovered dead, apparently murdered. A police dragnet was conducted, which eventually netted three Negro suspects. Confessions were needed. The first suspect was repeatedly hung from a tree by a deputy sheriff and, after being lowered, was tied to the tree and whipped into unconsciousness. The other two were taken to jail by the deputy sheriff, stripped, laid over chairs and cut to pieces with a leather strap with buckles on it. All three "confessed." They were immediately indicted and a trial was held the next day. At the trial, rope burns were clearly visible around the neck of the first suspect, and the other two were unable to sit. Hastily appointed counsel challenged these confessions (there was no other evidence against them) but was overruled by the judge; the jury convicted the three and sentenced them to death. The Supreme Court of Mississippi affirmed the convictions, holding that the admission into evidence of the confessions had not violated the defendants' constitutional rights. A Justice of the Mississippi Supreme Court entered a ringing dissent:

> . . . The so-called trial now before us . . . was never a
> legitimate proceeding from beginning to end; it was

never anything but a fictitious continuation of the mob which originally instituted and engaged in the admitted tortures. If this judgment be affirmed by the federal Supreme Court, it will be the first in the history of that court wherein there was allowed to stand a conviction based solely upon testimony coerced by the barbarities of executive officers of.the state, known to the prosecuting officers of the state as having been so coerced . . . and fully shown in all its nakedness to the trial judge. . . . The Scottsboro cases are models of correct constitutional procedure as compared with this now before the Court.

The Supreme Court could not ignore this cry for justice and, in a unanimous opinion authored by Chief Justice Hughes, and relying heavily on the dissent below. reversed the conviction. *Brown v. Mississippi,* 297 U.S. 278 (1936).

Although later cases to come to the Supreme Court presented police methods of lesser physical brutality, the principle that police should not use "third degree" methods to compel a person to incriminate himself continued to find applicability. Thus, in succeeding years, the Court reversed convictions based upon police methods which depended upon prolonged and repeated questioning, deprivation of sleep or food, and threats of bodily harm. Although these later cases did not involve actual beatings, there was such physical overbearing of the suspect by the police as to make inescapable the conclusion that the confession had been "compelled."

These reversals of convictions were founded upon sound policy considerations. There is a high risk of compelled confessions being false. Moreover, the drive for confessions provides police with an incentive to substitute brutality for scientific methods. And perhaps most important of all, "third degree" methods harden prisoners against society and lower public esteem for the administration of criminal justice. This last point—the preservation of the integrity of our system of criminal justice—was well put by that dissenting Mississippi judge:

It may be that in a rarely occasional case which

27

arouses the flaming indignation of a whole com-
munity, as was the case here, we shall continue yet for
a long time to have outbreaks of the mob or resorts to
its methods. But, if mobs and mob methods must
be, it would be better that their existence and their
methods shall be kept wholly separate from the
courts; that there shall be no blending of the devices of
the mob and of the proceedings of the courts; that
what the mob has so nearly completed let them
finish; and that no court shall by adoption give
legitimacy to any of the works of the mob, nor cover
by the frills and furbelows of a pretended legal trial·
the body of that which in fact is the product of the
mob, and then, by closing the eyes to actualities,
complacently adjudicate that the law of the land has
been observed and preserved.

This view of the peril to the integrity of the criminal process
in the use of coerced confessions was well put by Mr. Justice
Brandeis: "Crime is contagious. If the Government becomes a
lawbreaker it breeds contempt for law; it invites every man to
become a law unto himself; it invites anarchy. To declare that
in the administration of the criminal law the end justifies the
means ... would bring terrible retribution."

Having set its face against the police practice of coercing
confessions by physical mistreatment of prisoners, the Supreme
Court found itself unable to hold, as a matter of principle, that
the Fifth Amendment did not apply to confessions obtained by
police through psychological ploys. In a case decided by the
Supreme Court in 1959, the suspect had been held incommunicado at the police station for many hours. An old
friend, who was then a police trainee, entered the suspect's cell
and permitted him to make a telephone call. The "old friend"
then falsely told the suspect that permitting the telephone call
had gotten him into trouble with his superiors and that he
might be fired—with all the harmful effects that would have on
his wife and three children. Faced with the "old friend's"
entreaties—and unable to consult a lawyer—the suspect
signed a confession. The Supreme Court held that this

confession was "compelled" and reversed the conviction.

This process of defining the attributes of a "compelled" confession continued throughout the early 1960s in a series of cases before the Supreme Court. In these cases, factors such as incommunicado detention at the police station, denial of access to an attorney and police pressure upon the suspect's individual weaknesses or incapacities resulted in the invalidation of confessions. The whole process of custodial interrogation cried out for rationalization and, in 1966, in the landmark case of *Miranda v. Arizona,*[5] the Supreme Court attempted to do just that—to rationalize cases involving incommunicado interrogation of suspects in a police-dominated atmosphere for the purpose of securing evidence of their criminality with the Fifth Amendment's command that confessions not be "compelled."

The Court reviewed the normal incidents of such interrogation: isolation of the suspect; expressions of police confidence in his guilt; and persistent questioning. The Court explored various ploys like "Mutt and Jeff," in which one police officer (Mutt) talks tough to the suspect and makes various threats, while Jeff, out of Mutt's presence, suggests in a friendly way that it would be a good idea for him to confess and avoid the certain retribution Mutt has in store for him. Another ploy is the trick line-up in which a "witness" (actually a police agent) identifies the suspect as the man who committed the crime. A variation on this ploy is the reverse line-up, in which the "witness" picks the suspect out of a line-up as having committed other and more serious crimes, inducing the suspect to panic and "cooperate."

The Supreme Court reviewed all these routine incidents of station house questioning and found that they contained "inherently compelling pressures which work to undermine the individual's will to resist and to compel him to speak where he would not otherwise do so freely." The Court decided that some means must be devised to inform suspects of their right to silence and to assure a continuing opportunity to exercise it. Absent other means, the Court required that police, prior to

[5]384 U.S. 436 (1966) set forth as Appendix C.

questioning, give the suspect the following warnings in order to vouchsafe the suspect's privilege against self-incrimination:

1. That he has a right to remain silent;

2. That any statement he does make may be used as evidence against him;

3. That he has a right to the presence of an attorney; and,

4. That if he cannot afford an attorney, one will be appointed for him.

In 1964 the United States Supreme Court breathed new life into what before then had been a rarely used clause contained in the Sixth Amendment to the United States Constitution. It was in that year that the Court decided, in the case of *Escobedo v. Illinois,* 378 U.S. 902, that all accused persons have the right to the assistance of counsel, not only at trial but at every "critical stage" of a criminal proceeding.

Specifically, the Escobedo case holds that the refusal by the police to allow an accused person to consult with his lawyer during a police interrogation constitutes a denial of the Sixth Amendment's protection of the Assistance of Counsel. Since there was a denial of Sixth Amendment rights, a confession that the Chicago police obtained during the interrogation of Escobedo was held to be inadmissible. The Escobedo case dealt a deathblow to what was once formally known (and accepted) as the protracted "third degree."

In both *Miranda* and in the *Escobedo* cases the Supreme Court determined that police in-custody interrogation is also a critical stage of a criminal proceeding, and that the guiding hand of counsel was essential to protect Mirand's warnings—the prerequisite to a valid waiver of the Fifth Amendment rights— are heavily laden with reminders about the right to counsel. If police do not give the Miranda warnings or attempt to give the accused the full benefit of consulting with his or her attorney or an appointed one, the confession violates both the Fifth and Sixth Amendments and is inadmissible.

An out-of-court identification of an accused in a police-controlled lineup is also a critical stage of a criminal prosecution where the accused has the undiluted right to counsel. The

Supreme Court has emphasized that there is a grave likelihood of preconditioning identification witnesses—whether intentionally or not—that requires the safeguard of an attorney for the accused at the lineup. Police must notify an accused person's lawyer of the time and place of the lineup and must do everything possible to preserve fairness of procedures at the lineup.

Recent enforcement by the Supreme Court of the privilege against self-incrimination and the right to counsel has brought upon its head a wealth of scorn and abuse. But anyone who traces the gradual explication and evolution of these constitutional rights will be unable to accept the charge that the Court has abandoned restraint. In fact, what the Court has done has been to make the Bill of Rights a meaningful protection of citizens from every part of American life.

Chapter 6
UNCONSTITUTIONAL POLICE PRACTICES: REMEDIES

Previous chapters have tried to define the individual's rights which the police are obliged by the Bill of Rights to respect. But what are the citizen's remedies if the police violate these rights? What can he do if the police stop him from making a lawful speech or handing out political leaflets? What can he do if the police arrest him under a vague and open-ended law? What can he do if the police arrest him without an arrest warrant or search him without a search warrant, under circumstances in which the warrant requirement is not excused? What can he do if the police coerce a confession from him? Finally, what can he do if the police use excessive force upon him?

The most common remedy is the so-called exclusionary rule, which comes into play when the police attempt to use a product of their unconstitutional conduct to convict the individual. The Supreme Court has held that products (whether direct or indirect) of illegal police conduct—whether personal belongings, admissions or even fingerprints—are to be excluded from evidence at the individual's criminal trial. Thus, if an illegal arrest or search or wiretap turns up, say, narcotics or an incriminating conversation, the prosecutor cannot use it as evidence or even to obtain leads to other evidence.

This exclusionary rule was developed and enforced by the Supreme Court only after decades of experience with illegal police conduct. Although the exclusionary rule had been employed in federal trials since the early 1900s, the Supreme Court had refrained from applying it to state trials in the hope that state authorities would develop an alternative remedy to restrain and deter the police from engaging in unconstitutional practices. By 1961, in the famous case of *Mapp v. Ohio*, the Court was compelled to sadly confess that the states had not developed adequate remedies to protect the individual's rights and that the imposition of the exclusionary rule was necessary.

In *Mapp,* the Court traced the constitutional development of the right to privacy free from unreasonable state intrusion and concluded that it was necessary "to close the only courtroom door remaining open to evidence secured by official law-lessness.... We hold that all evidence obtained by searches and seizures in violation of the Constitution is, by that same authority, inadmissible in a state court." In applying the exclusionary rule to the States, the Court reasoned: *81-139 42*

> The ignoble shortcut to conviction left open to the State tends to destroy the entire system of constitutional restraints on which the liberties of the people rest. Having once recognized that the right to privacy embodied in the Fourth Amendment is enforceable against the States, and that the right to be secure against rude invasions of privacy by state officers is, therefore, constitutional in origin, we can no longer permit that right to remain an empty promise.... Our decision ... gives to the individual no more than that which the Constitution guarantees him, to the police officer no less than that to which honest law enforcement is entitled, and, to the courts, that judicial integrity so necessary in the true administration of justice.

But the exclusionary rule is not without its problems and pitfalls. Let us consider an example. A criminal defendant believes the evidence the prosecutor intends to use against him has been secured by an illegal wiretap. Before he can take advantage of the exclusionary rule, he must hurdle four barriers. First, he must prove the existence of the wiretap. Second, he must show that the wiretap was either on his phone or picked up his conversation. Third, he must show that the wiretap was illegal. And fourth, he must show that the illegal wiretap yielded something which the prosecution is using against him at trial.

But these issues pale in comparison to a much larger one: the problem of police lying. This phenomenon is well known among members of the Bar and the police. In a ludicrously high number of cases, the police have overcome a defendant's motion to suppress illegally seized narcotics by testifying that the defendant, when approached by the police officers, reached into his pocket, dropped the narcotics on the ground and attempted to flee. This is popularly known as the "dropsie" habit and has happened so often, if police testimony is to be believed, as to be a well recognized addictive characteristic.

Another remedy which an individual might employ is to bring a civil action for damages against the offending officer. Thus, if the individual is subjected to an illegal arrest or search or excessive force, he may sue the officer for damages. Although this remedy sounds good in theory, in practice it has proven unworkable. Indeed, the unworkability of this remedy was one of the reasons which led the Supreme Court to conclude that the imposition of the exclusionary rule on the states was necessary. The reasons for the unworkability of this remedy are practical and many. The individual must hire a lawyer, often an expense which he cannot afford. These suits are not popular among most lawyers, because they are messy, controversial and hard to win. Such a lawsuit becomes a swearing contest between the individual and the police in which, experience has shown, the individual will win out in only clear cases.

Consider a case of police brutality. The law is clear that even if an individual has done something to justify a legal arrest or search, he must not be subjected to excessive police force. Experience teaches, however, that policeman often see their roles as something of a father substitute, in which they can summarily deal out corporal punishment to a wrongdoer. In order to cover themselves, policemen who dispense such corporal punishment routinely press a charge of assault or resisting arrest, so as to discourage the individual from bringing a civil lawsuit. As has been documented, these criminal charges are only a hedge by the police against such a lawsuit. Since police usually win swearing contests in the lower criminal courts, the conviction will be useful to the police defensively against any civil lawsuit against them. This has led some members of the Bar to facetiously coin a new crime, namely, "resisting assault."

Neither of the remedies discussed above—the exclusionary rule or a civil action for damages—gets at the root problem of an unconstitutional arrest. A root solution would ensure that the next time a person was making a speech or picketing or just having a moment of peace and quiet on his stoop, he would not be subjected to arrest. If the problem could be accurately diagnosed as stemming from an overwhelmingly large number of malicious policemen, then an effective remedy would be nothing less than a complete overhauling of the recruitment and training methods of the police. But the problem is not centrally one of police maliciousness, since, fortunately, malicious cops are the exception and not the rule. The real problem goes deeper. Its source is in the vague and open-ended laws and police regulations which give policemen a sense of power much greater than that which the Constitution allows. The remedy must be coextensive with the wrong, and must include the power to eradicate those legal weapons in the police arsenal which the police employ to deprive citizens of their rights.

In recent years, federal courts have developed just such a remedy—the invalidation of state criminal laws which, by their grant of too much discretion to the police, constitute a major source of abusive police conduct.

Chapter 7

POLICE METHODS AND PRACTICES: ARREST

Arrest with a Warrant

An arrest must be made for the purpose of bringing the person before the proper court, body or official.

The arrestor is required to make known his intention to arrest. He is not required, however, to run the risk of thereby endangering himself or the making of the arrest where the person to be arrested is of a known bad character. If the arrest is under a warrant, he should make known his possession of it and the nature of the charges; if not under the warrant, he should make known the offense for which it is made. This is not necessary if the arrestee, knowing him to be an officer, does not request the information.

An arrest may, however, be made at any time providing the warrant has not lapsed, and providing it is not at an unreasonable time when made for a misdemeanor or for a civil case. An arrest in a civil process may never be made on Sunday or at night unless the process so authorizes.

Each state has enacted its own laws governing issuance of warrants, and there are many technical variations, yet the basic requirements remain the same in all material respects.

WARRANT MUST BE FAIR ON ITS FACE: A warrant may be fair on its face and yet not necessarily valid. It is then said to have latent, as distinguished from patent defects. Such a warrant is apparently regular in form, but may have been issued by some court or official not having authority to issue warrants covering the conduct for which it is issued, but having authority to issue warrants for conduct similar to that described. Or the court or official issuing it may not have jurisdiction over the person named or described, but the facts stated in the warrant are such that, if they really existed, would confer jurisdiction; or the proceedings required for the proper issuance may not have been complied with, but there is nothing in the warrant to indicate this. But one serving a warrant is expected to know the formal requirements of a valid warrant and should inspect it to see if all the facts that must appear are stated therein.

If the person serving the warrant knows some fact which does not appear on the face, the existence of which would make the warrant invalid, he will not be liable for damages for effecting the arrest.

On the other hand, if the warrant on its face describes any such facts, or if the proper steps necessary for its issuance have not been taken, he will be held for damages for the false arrest. But, in any case, a person who serves a warrant must know the jurisdiction of the court issuing it and if it has no authority to issue *any* warrants, the paper purporting to be a warrant which was issued by it, will not protect the server from liability. If the court only has authority to issue warrants for particular offenses, the officer serving it must know its limited scope and may not make an arrest for any other offense. For example, if the court is a juvenile court given jurisdiction over offenses committed by persons under 18, if the warrant on its face shows that the person to be arrested is over that age, not only is the arrest invalid, but the officer is liable for damages. Or the statute may provide that the prosecution for the particular offense is to be initiated by *summons.* Any warrant issued to arrest for that offense is invalid and cannot protect the officer serving it.

An officer must also know the extent to which State or Federal Constitutions limit the power of the government to confer jurisdiction on the issuing body. If an action is one exclusively within the jurisdiction of the federal courts, a state court may not issue a warrant.

It is, however, only necessary that the crime for which the warrant is issued be of the same general character as that for which the court has authority to issue warrants. The officer is not required to know, for example, whether the conduct for which it was issued constitutes a crime. He can rely on the judge's signature to the effect that it is.

WARRANT MUST BE ISSUED BY COURT HAVING JURISDICTION OVER A PERSON SUFFICIENTLY NAMED: A prime requirement is that the person intended be sufficiently named. A warrant is always valid even though the person sought to be arrested is in fact innocent of the offense for which he is charged. A warrant is invalid, however, if the person to be arrested is not sufficiently named. If the arrestor, making a reasonable error, arrests some person other than the one named, the arrest is not privileged and he will be liable for damages. And the converse is also true—the fact that, though the warrant does not sufficiently describe him, the officer, by some stroke of luck, arrests the person actually intended, does not thereby validate the arrest. However, there, too, one must remember that if the officer could arrest legally without out a warrant, and if he gives notice that he is also arresting on suspicion, the defect will be cured. If the name of the person is not known, an adequate description will suffice.

If there are two persons with the same name, the arrest of the wrong one will not be legal, but if the officer used due diligence and arrested the one he honestly and reasonably believed to be intended, he cannot be held for damages. On the other hand, if the intended arrestee goes by two names, the use of either one in the warrant is sufficient. Since the officer is under a duty to serve warrants, in the case where there is some mixup in names, it is reasonable for him to rely on the name given in the warrant unless he actually knows a mistake has been made. And even though he may have reason to suspect a mistake in naming the proper person, he may arrest under the warrant the person to whom the name in the warrant applies without thereby incurring civil liability.

But he will be liable for arresting a person accurately named if he knows beyond a reasonable doubt that he is not the person intended. In such a case, if the *description* of the person actually intended is sufficient, though some-one else is named, he may arrest the one described. The officer should always keep in mind that if he does not believe the person named is the person intended, he makes the arrest of the person named at his peril. If the description or name could fit two people, in determining which is intended, he should take into consideration the respective reputation of each. If one is of unimpeachable reputation, he would be wise to refrain from arresting him without a thorough investigation.

If the name of the person to be arrested is unknown, the warrant should so state and then any description that will serve to identify him properly is sufficient.

POSSESSION OF WARRANT: If an arrest is made, and the officer arresting does not have the warrant in his possession at the time, the arrest will be viewed by the courts in the same light as if it were made without a war-rant. The fact that the person arrested did not ask to see the warrant or did not know that it had not been issued does not appear to effect the outcome. The party to be arrested, if the arrest is for the type of misdemeanor for which arrest without a warrant is illegal, may resist the arrest, and the arrestor may be guilty of assault if he per-sists in the attempt. These rules also hold where a sheriff deputizes someone.

Arrest without a Warrant

The rules regarding arrest on procurement of a warrant are simple and concise. When we come to the field of arrest without a warrant, which applies to both officers and private persons, there exist some areas of doubt as to just what the rule is in a particular jurisdiction.

COMMON LAW RULES: Under the common law, which existed prior to the enactment of legislation by most states, an officer and a private citizen had, with one or two exceptions, nearly the same power in effecting an arrest without a warrant. A peace officer or a private citizen both could arrest to prevent the commission of treason, a felony or a breach of the peace; or while such acts were in the process of commission; or after the treason or felony were committed. Arrest without a warrant *after* the commission of a breach of the peace, was permitted only if it was committed in the arrestor's presence and only if followed by immediate and continuous pursuit.

If a felony or treason had actually been committed, and the defendant was suspect, he could be arrested if "reasonable grounds" for the suspicion existed. If no felony was actually committed by anyone, but a peace officer had reasonable grounds to believe that the defendant had committed one, he could arrest, but a private citizen could not. There could be no arrest without a warrant for any misdemeanor except a breach of the peace.

It can be seen from the foregoing that there would be little difficulty if either the police officer or the private citizen had witnessed the commission of an act of treason, a felony or a breach of the peace, or if either stepped in to prevent the commission of one of these crimes. Problems arise, however, when a policeman or private citizen arriving on the scene, are told that robbers have just left a store with a big haul. One robber is described as bald-headed, wearing a plaid overcoat and walking with a limp. Dashing into the street, you spy a man answering that description loitering in the vicinity of the crime and promptly announce, "You are under arrest." Let us suppose he is actually the "stranger" who was in the store when the gems disappeared. However, they turn out not to have been stolen by anyone, but merely taken out by a partner to be appraised. But the stranger had acted so queerly as to create a suspicion that he was taking something. What about the legality of the arrest? There were "reasonable grounds" to believe the arrestee guilty, but no felony was actually committed. Under the common law rule, if you are a police officer, the arrest is legal, but if you are a private citizen, there can be unpleasant consequences for being wrong. You may have used force to effect the arrest and injured the arrestee or an innocent third party so that you have incurred liability.

40

Or suppose there really was a robbery but it was dark and an excited witness gave an erroneous description of the culprit. What about the legality of the arrest of someone answering the description found three blocks away? Or a mile away from the scene of the crime? Is it "reasonable grounds" to rely on the testimony of the eyewitness? And what if you knew the only witness had notoriously bad eyesight? And what is the effect on reasonableness of the distance of the arrester from the scene of the crime? Or of whether he is apprehended 10 minutes later or one hour later? Here a felony has actually been committed, but are your grounds for suspecting the defendant reasonable? A jury which may have to decide the question must ask how a normal reasonable man would react in the same circumstances and judge the reasonableness of the arrest accordingly.

There is no yardstick to aid an officer in the performance of his duty for determining in each case whether he had reasonable grounds for his suspicions. It is enough if the circumstances which he knows or reasonably believes to exist are such as to create a reasonable belief that there is a likelihood that the felony has been committed and that the one arrested committed it.

The misdemeanor-arrest rule causes the most trouble, particularly to the private citizen. He knows that murder is a felony and that spitting on the sidewalk is a misdemeanor, but when we get down to something like shoplifting, he isn't sure which it is, or whether the value of the goods stolen has any effect on the degree of the crime. Even the officer is often in the same predicament because many things are labelled felony that are less serious than many misdemeanors, and some things that he may think are felonies, are not. Both had better be right. Under many of the statutes though, an officer may only arrest without a warrant for a misdemeanor committed in his presence, or for one that is a breach of the peace and a private citizen may never arrest for a misdemeanor. A peculiar quirk in the way this common law rule operated was that if the officer had no reasonable grounds to believe the defendant guilty of a felony when he arrested him, but if he did in fact turn out to be guilty, the arrest was not legal. An officer might arrest a disreputable character out of spite or in order to question him, and it might turn out on a search of his person that he was in fact guilty of the felony of carrying a concealed weapon, but the arrest does not thereby become legal. And, as we shall see later, the search of a person made in connection with an illegal arrest is not legal.

ARREST STATUTES: *Arrest by private person*—The common law rules (discussed above) are important to us today because they are still the law in many states. In a few jurisdictions, for example, the right of private persons to make arrests without a warrant has been extended to cases where any misdemeanor, not just a breach of the peace, is committed in his presence. By and large, however, this right to arrest for misdemeanors is not granted by statute and must be sought in the common law.

There are often provisions giving defined classes of peace officers such as representatives of the A. S. P. C. A. the right to arrest for certain specified offenses. As regards all other offenses, they have only the same rights as private citizens.

There appear to be few statutory provisions which change the common law rules with regard to rights of a private person to arrest for a felony. His rights are still limited to arrest for a felony *actually* committed where he has reasonable grounds to suspect the person arrested of being the guilty party, or to prevent the commission of a felony or where one has actually been committed in his presence.

Arrest by officer for felony—Most statutory provisions increase the right of officers to make arrests. Thus, under the statutes an officer may arrest for a misdemeanor committed in his presence, other than a breach of peace, as well as for a felony. Another change is that he may also arrest when the person arrested has actually committed a felony though not in the officer's presence, regardless of whether the officer believes he has done so. If a felony has been committed and he has reasonable grounds to believe that

42

the person arrested committed it, or if he has reasonable grounds to believe that a felony has been or is being committed and reasonable grounds to believe that the person to be arrested has committed or is committing it, he may arrest under the statute as well as at common law. Provisions of this nature have been adopted in at least 16 states. This type of statute protects an officer who makes a mistake of law, as for example, when he believes the statute makes the act committed a felony but he is in error.

Arrest by officer for misdemeanor—There are some special statutes which give an officer the right to arrest for certain special misdemeanors not committed in his presence, but in the absence of such a statute or a statute generally giving the right to arrest for misdemeanors committed in his presence, the officer must rely on his common law right to arrest for only those misdemeanors that are breaches of the peace. The exception is made for breaches of the peace because, particularly where they involve fighting and affrays, a very dangerous situation can be created whereby many persons can be seriously hurt. Where a breach of the peace is occurring, the officer, as distinguished from the private citizen, need not actually see the person arrested participating in the breach. He may arrest all apparent as well as actual participants.

There are six states in which the courts have indicated that there may be arrests by officers for any misdemeanors committed in their presence without a warrant—Washington, Missouri, Kansas, New Jersey, Pennsylvania and Virginia. The federal courts have also so held in regard to arrests by federal officers, even where the offense does not amount to a breach of the peace. Several states have recently enacted statutory provisions to this effect.

SPECIAL SITUATIONS: *Aiding officer in effecting arrest*—A private citizen may not be inclined to make an arrest without a warrant on his own, but he may, at one time or another, be called on by someone whom he knows to be an officer to aid in effecting an arrest or in recapturing an escaped prisoner. If he is sure it is an officer he is aiding, he can not be held responsible for damages if the officer is exceeding his authority, though Massachusetts and New York have held contrary. However, he acts at his own risk if the person he is aiding is not really an officer or is a special officer with limited authority. On the other hand, many states make it a misdemeanor for a citizen to refuse to help when called upon. To be fully protected, the citizen must be acting in the presence of the officer, that is, in the same vicinity, though they need not be visible to each other.

Breaking down doors to effect arrest—Though it is true that anyone acting under a warrant may, if necessary, to accomplish the arrest, break down doors and search the house for the offender, he may only do so if a necessity exists and he has given notice of his purpose and authority. The same rules apply when arresting without a warrant providing the arrester is acting within his lawful right. It should be noted therefore, that although an officer may break down doors to arrest for a felony or to suppress a breach of the peace, a private citizen may only do so to prevent the commission or continuance of a felony. Even the officer, in the absence of a statute granting the right to arrest for all misdemeanors, would need a warrant if the breach of the peace for which he seeks to arrest was not committed in his presence and he is not engaging in a "fresh pursuit." "Breaking" is defined as turning door knobs, lifting latches, pushing open or unfastening a window and like show of force. Where an escape after arrest is involved, an officer immediately pursuing may, where the arrest was for a felony, break down doors without a warrant and without stopping to give prior notice of his purpose and without demanding admission.

Neither a private citizen nor an officer may, without a warrant, break doors to arrest for a misdemeanor even though they have reasonable grounds to suspect it is being committed within. However, this does not apply where the officer knows, as evidenced by his own senses, that a breach of the peace is taking place.

44

Arrest of insane person or drunk—An insane person dangerous to himself or others may be arrested and detained a reasonable time, by an officer or a citizen without a warrant, when there is a reasonable necessity to prevent immediate injury to himself or others, but not otherwise. The one making the arrest acts at the peril of being able to prove insanity or dangerous character. However, a few states such as New York, Oklahoma, North Dakota, South Dakota, Montana and Washington have modified this rule by statute. In a section dealing with assaults that are justified, the statutes permit the use of force in enforcing such restraint against a person temporarily or partially deprived of reason as is necessary for the protection of the person or his restoration to health during the period necessary to obtain legal authority for restraint or custody. This amounts to a limited right for anyone to arrest such a person until some court order can be obtained.

The above provision has been invoked to arrest drunks. However, many states have statutes specifically dealing with the arrest of drunks with or without a warrant.

Arrest of members of armed forces—Formerly, no private citizen could arrest a member of the armed forces, hence a deserter could not be arrested civilly. Now, by statute and the Articles of War, civil officers having authority by the laws of the United States or of the states to make arrests generally, may arrest deserters, and no warrant is necessary.

Use of Force in Effecting Arrest or Recapture

The arrester, whether an officer or a private person, may use such force as is necessary to effect the arrest or recapture or to maintain custody of the person arrested. But what do we mean by "necessary"? What is *actually* necessary; what the arrester believed to be necessary; or what a normal reasonable man, if standing in the arrester's shoes, would believe to be necessary on the basis of the facts known to him?

An officer, about to make an arrest, is told he may use such force as is necessary to effect the arrest and that he may not use his gun except as a last resort. Beyond that, he is provided with little in the way of an objective standard. If he is not too fleet of foot, when pursuing one who is evading capture, will he be justified in shooting sooner than his more agile comrades? Or, if he is five-foot-five, does that give him the right to "draw" quicker when engaged in an unequal scuffle with a bandit who is six-foot-four than if he were struggling with a woman or a midget? And must he take into consideration other factors such as the presence of fellow officers or of bystanders that he might call upon? And is the nature of the offense committed material? Certainly, what becomes necessary force when dealing with a trigger happy four-time loser may not be held necessary when arresting for a minor traffic violation. To the rookie cop, faced for the first time with the necessity of making split-second decisions such as those indicated, to be judged by 12 men, tried and true, sitting *eons later* in a safe jury box and with time and opportunity galore to weigh the pros and cons of the situation, must seem manifestly unfair. It is for this reason that it is generally held that his actions need not be right, merely reasonable.

USE OF FORCE IN ARRESTING FOR FELONY: It is customary to find that the rules are couched in terms of the nature of the offense which has been or is being committed. Since the law differs in respect to whether we are dealing with a felony or a misdemeanor, the arrester is in the awkward position of having to determine, in the first instance, into which category the offense fits. The issue is not too vital if the person seeking to arrest is an officer with a warrant and the offense committed is murder. However, it is crucial if the person arresting is a private person and the offense is one of the "borderline" cases which could logically fit into either category. If it is a misdemeanor, the person under the law of the particular jurisdiction, may have no rights whatsoever to arrest without a warrant, so that not only is he liable civilly for the false arrest, but also, since any force he uses thereby becomes excessive, for criminal assault as well. However, the arrester who seeks to use force to effect the arrest must consider two things—first, whether the arrest itself is lawful, and second, that he uses no more force than has usually been considered reasonable for effecting an arrest for that sort of offense.

But must the felony have actually been committed by the person to be arrested or is it enough if the officer reasonably believes that it has? Holding that reasonable grounds for suspicion are sufficient are California, Washington, Massachusetts, Maryland, Georgia, Tennessee, Oklahoma, Virginia, North Carolina and probably Florida. By statute, South Carolina, New Hampshire and Rhode Island achieve this same result. This is the majority view and a sensible one, though if the officer is wrong, there may be tragic results. Holding that the officer acts at his peril and must be right in his suspicions are Kentucky, Pennsylvania, West Virginia and possibly Arizona. By statute, Alaska and Oregon arrive at the same result, and the statutes of New York Minnesota and Nevada seem to require that a felony must actually have been committed by someone, though not necessarily by the arrestee.

The distinctions made by the law are twofold: (1) if force likely to produce death is used, it may only be lawful in effecting an arrest for certain types of offenses, namely felony, and (2) the amount of force to be used may be dependent upon the nature of the resistance offered to arrest, whether it consists merely of flight or of struggling with the arrester. At some point, in the latter instance, if the arrester persists in his attempt to arrest as he is justified in doing, he may find his life in danger, at which time he becomes justified in the use of greater force than heretofore.

RIGHT TO USE FORCE AGAINST FELON FLEEING ARREST: At common law, an officer could kill to overcome any resistance to arrest by a felon, including flight. There was a great deal of logic to the rule because at common law all felonies were punishable by death. But now, where the death sentence has been abolished everywhere for all but a few of the offenses which we designate felonies, it is rather an anachronism to say that a man who could be

47

sentenced at the most to a few years in prison for an offense, can justifiably be shot by a policeman before there is even any proof of his guilt and merely because he runs away. Yet it is generally the rule that deadly force may be used where a fleeing felon cannot otherwise be captured. The common law, however, required that there exist a reasonable necessity to use such force. This meant that the officer had to satisfy the jury that he tried in good faith and with reasonable prudence and caution to make the arrest and resisted the employment of severe means until, as determined by the state of things between them, the arrest could not otherwise be made. Usually what appears to be reasonably necessary will be held sufficient.

What is reasonable necessity? The factors to be considered in determining what is reasonable necessity are whether the officer made his official character known, particularly where he was not in uniform, whether he warned that he would use force or fired warning shots before shooting to kill, and whether he made reasonable efforts to capture by pursuing. Was the situation such that, with some additional effort on the officer's part, the felon could have been overtaken?

Once the arrestee has offered to surrender, or is helpless from wounds, or the officer is in a position to call on other officers nearby or possibly on bystanders for help, there is no longer any necessity to shoot. He must exercise considerable discretion though, and if a risk to innocent bystanders will ensue from the use of deadly force, or he knows that he will have ample opportunity to capture the culprit at some future date, these factors may militate against the necessity to use force.

For example, if the officer knows that the felon will be cut off at the point towards which he is heading by fellow officers, or that escape will be impossible for one of a number of reasons, there is no necessity to shoot. However, if the person to be arrested had been known in the past to resist arrest violently when cornered, this factor may point towards necessity. The character of the felon and of the crime which he has committed are relevant. The officer may also be permitted to take into consideration the fact that the arrestee is fast approaching a very advantageous position from which he can seek cover and harm his pursuers.

Statutory treatment—New Hampshire and Rhode Island have adopted the Uniform Arrest Act which requires that a reasonable necessity to use deadly force exist.

It is to be noted that nearly all the provisions regarding the right of an officer to use force in effecting arrest are to be found, oddly enough, not in the sections granting the right to arrest, but in the Justifiable Homicide provisions. Listed under homicides for which the law exacts no penalty, we find killing by an officer in effecting an arrest. In all but a very few states the requirement of necessity to kill does not appear in the statute but is a holdover from the common law of arrest.

There are a few states which, by judicial decision, seem to require that there be an *absolute* necessity, as distinguished from reasonable necessity, before deadly force may be used. They are Alabama, New York, Kentucky and probably Tennessee. Such a strict standard is very hard on the officer who must make the decision but grants greater protection to the individual than any other. It is to be remembered that, though it may be a hardened criminal now seeking to escape, the next time it may be an innocent victim.

PRIVATE PERSON'S RIGHT TO USE FORCE: There are few statutes specifically dealing with the right of a private person to use force in effectuating an arrest. Florida, Mississippi, New Mexico, North Dakota, Oklahoma, South Dakota and Wisconsin provide that homicide committed by "any person in attempting by lawful ways and means to apprehend any person for any felony committed . . ." is justified.

In North Carolina and Pennsylvania it has been held that a private person may not shoot a fleeing felon, where the felon was of minor or non-atrocious nature. It is the rule pretty generally that a private person may not use deadly force where the felony is not of the atrocious kind even though it seemed reasonably necessary to prevent his escape. Texas, by statute, makes an exception if the offense is committed at nighttime where the identity of the felon may be unknown and hence subsequent arrest difficult or impossible.

Right to Use Force Against Misdemeanant

Though the officer may kill a fleeing felon he may never, under any circumstances, kill a fleeing misdemeanant. This puts the onus on the officer to know which category the particular offense fits. The attempted use of deadly force against the misdemeanant subjects the arrester to civil and criminal penalties and opens the door for the person fleeing to shoot back in self-defense. There are, however, a few states which have enacted statutory provisions that justify the use of deadly force in such a case, namely, Hawaii, California and Missouri.

Where the offense is only a misdemeanor, flight or resistance will never justify infliction of a dangerous wound to effect an arrest. It is immaterial whether the acts occur before arrest or afterwards in an attempted escape. However, if the struggle is unduly prolonged, a point may be reached in which the life of the arrester is endangered. It is then said that neither a private person nor an officer attempting a valid arrest loses his right to self-defense. In arresting for misdemeanor, he is under no duty to retreat or abandon the arrest. Therefore, unless the misdemeanant breaks away at some point before the arrester's life is endangered, the latter may ultimately be permitted to shoot in self-defense.

In effecting an arrest for a misdemeanor, there are decisions in the following states—Arkansas, Indiana, Iowa, Illinois, Mississippi, New Mexico, New York, Oklahoma, Pennsylvania, Tennessee and Texas—which justify killing only in self-defense. There are, however, a few other states, namely, Alabama, Georgia, Hawaii, Kentucky, Missouri, North Carolina and Wisconsin where the courts permit killing to overcome the misdemeanant's resistance though the arrester is in no great danger.

In many states, the language of the statutes would imply that killing to overcome a misdemeanant's resistance is justified, but they have not been so interpreted by the courts, and it would be extremely unwise to rely on them to this effect in any states other than Hawaii, Missouri and Wisconsin. The statutes divide themselves roughly into two groups. The first type authorizes the use of all necessary means to compel arrest when under authority of a warrant or after notice, if the arrestee "either flee or forcibly resist." Alaska, Arizona, California, Hawaii, Idaho, Indiana, Minnesota, Missouri, Tennessee and Utah have this type of statute. The second type is less general and applies only to homicides which are declared justifiable when necessarily committed in overcoming *actual resistance* to the execution of some legal process or in the discharge of any other legal duty. This provision appears in the Codes of Arizona, California, Florida, Montana, North Dakota, New Mexico, Oklahoma, Oregon, South Dakota, Utah, Vermont and Wisconsin. It is to be noted that a few states have both types. A similar justifiable homicide provision is to be found in Arkansas, Colorado, Illinois, Minnesota, Nevada and New York.

Self-Defense Generally

Implicit in the doctrine of self-defense is the requirement that the use of deadly force be reasonably necessary. Any assault on one's person will not justify the use of more force than would be required to terminate the attack. Consequently, any feeble struggling on the part of a physically inferior arrestee will not justify his opponent in pulling a gun in "self-defense." It must also be kept in mind that in every instance, the use of excessive force may subject the user to a suit for damages. In determining the reasonableness of the killing, all of the factors previously discussed will be considered, i.e., that there are several officers against one criminal, that the latter is apparently getting the worst of the struggle, and so forth. Preparation of a chart showing all of the factors going to establish unreason-ableness is an impossibility. No two combinations of factors are ever identical and the facts in each case must be weighed and judged on the individual merits.

Yet the impression is not meant to be left that a resisting felon may only be killed in self-defense. Though that is generally the rule where misdemeanors are involved, in the case of resisting felons, there exists a privilege, apart from the right to self-defense, to use deadly force where neces-sary to effect the arrest. The arrester, being under no duty to desist from attempting to arrest when the resistance is great, may find himself in the position, though his life is not endangered, where he must either draw a weapon or abandon the arrest. He is perfectly justified in doing the former providing, as in the case of the fleeing felon, he is reasonable in his belief that a necessity to do so exists.

Penalty for Illegal Use of Force

If the arrester uses an excessive amount of force in ar-resting, maintaining custody or recapturing, that is, more than is reasonably necessary, he will be liable civilly for damages. He will, also, as we shall see, subject himself to recriminatory force, for the arrestee now has a privilege to defend himself. If the arrester has the right to arrest another, he may use such force against the other or against any third person who interferes, which is the same amount of force as he was privileged to use in effecting the arrest.

After the arrest, if any force is used against a non-resisting prisoner, the arrester is liable for any damages resulting from his abusive conduct. This includes failure to turn the arrestee over promptly to the custody of the proper officials.

Resistance to Arrest, When Justified

Most of what has been said about the subject of arrest, up to this point, is only of interest to officers of the law. Let us now examine the problem from the standpoint of the person being arrested.

No one has any lawful right to resist a lawful arrest made

in a lawful manner, and an intentional killing perpetrated in the course of such resistance is murder. An unintentional killing of the arrester, occuring as a result of the resistance, has not uniformly been held to be murder, but the lightest the arrestee may hope to get off with is a manslaughter charge.

ILLEGAL ARREST, GENERALLY: Though much can be said for the opposite viewpoint, the rule pretty generally accepted is that one may resist an unlawful arrest though only one's liberty be at stake, and though no force has been used by the arrester. New Hampshire has by statute adopted Section 6 of the Uniform Arrest Act which makes it a duty to submit to any arrest, even an illegal one. The rationale behind this attempt to change the prevailing law is that an illegal arrest can be peaceably rectified at the station house, so that no justification exists to take the law into one's own hands to obtain release.

The question of the extent of the privilege to forcibly resist an unlawful arrest can arise in one of four ways—either when an officer with a void warrant or without any warrant attempts an illegal arrest or when a private citizen, under the same circumstances, attempts to do the same thing.

BY UNKNOWN OFFICER: In the case of an officer acting without a warrant, the distinction is sometimes made on the basis of whether he is a known officer or not, and if he is not, the attempted illegal arrest constitutes an assault which may be resisted. The arrestee may, if he is so disposed, use whatever force is reasonably necessary to escape, short of taking the life of his assailant. Of course, he must keep in mind what a jury will think is necessary when he acts. Where his life is not threatened, it is safe to say that he will not usually be considered justified in using a deadly weapon. By this it is not meant to imply that the use of such a weapon is *per se* unlawful and the question of the reasonableness of its use under the particular circumstances is for the jury to decide. However, where his life is endangered by the acts of the officer, he may kill if reasonably necessary to save it. South Carolina, Nebraska and possibly Texas permit killing of an unknown officer merely to regain one's liberty. A pretty high price to place on a man's freedom! Bear in mind, however, that if the officer is known, all states require submission to the illegal arrest if they make any distinction at all between known and unknown officers.

The vast majority of states make no distinction based on whether the officer is known or not and they hold that when he exceeds his authority, he loses the protection of the law and may be resisted.

VOID WARRANT: An officer, acting under a void warrant, acts at his peril. The arrestee may use any force short of taking life, that is reasonably necessary to regain his liberty. In some states, a killing in the course of resisting arrest under a void warrant is held to be manslaughter on the theory that the officer's unlawful conduct "provoked" the arrestee, thereby reducing the degree of the crime. This theory is untenable if we remember that, particularly in the case of a latent defect in the warrant, the arrestee may not even suspect the invalidity. New Mexico and Georgia have arrived at the happy compromise that where it can be shown that he was justifiably provoked, that is, he knew of the illegality of the arrest, it is manslaughter. Otherwise, it is murder just like any other killing for which no acceptable excuse exists. Most states hold that the murder charge will be reduced to manslaughter if heat and passion leading up to the killing can be shown.

Where the arrest is being made by a private citizen, the law regarding the right to resist an illegal arrest is the same. Where a distinction is made between officers that are known and those that are not, the case of the private citizen is treated in the same manner as if he were an unknown officer.

Patent defect in the warrant—While many jurisdictions make no distinctions between arrest under a warrant with a patent defect and one with a latent defect, there are others that do. In one type of patent defect, where the warrant is executed outside of the jurisdiction of the issuing court, it is an absolute nullity and affords the officer no protection. Texas goes so far as to hold that such an officer even loses his right to kill in self-defense. This is not the law elsewhere, however, and it is usually held that if an officer relies on a defective warrant, even though the defect is apparent on the face, he will not lose his right to self-defense when threatened with severe harm by the arrestee. And if he is held to have killed in self-defense, he will not be guilty of even manslaughter, the homicide being one in the class which is considered justified. But this is true only of an actual self-defense situation. If he kills, not to protect his own life, but to effect the illegal arrest, he has no such privilege.

Latent defect in the warrant—Where the defect in the warrant is latent, that is, does not appear on its face, most jurisdictions hold, and rightly so, that a defect, of which the killer had no knowledge, cannot be a mitigating circumstance to reduce the degree of the crime. And those states that do not distinguish between the types of defects hold that a homicide, committed while resisting an illegal arrest under such a warrant, cannot be more than manslaughter in the absence of a showing of express malice. They can justify such a holding only because they recognize no real difference between a defect which the arrestee can see and therefore knows to render the warrant illegal and one of which he can have no knowledge. In most jurisdictions, if a warrant appears fair on its face, a person who kills in resisting its execution can be held for murder. The fact that the officer knew some facts that might tend to invalidate it does not seem to be material.

Chapter 8

POLICE METHODS AND PRACTICES:
SEARCH AND SEIZURE

A search may be legal for one of three or four reasons, either because it is conducted under a search warrant validly issued, or because it is incidental to a lawful arrest, or it is based on probable cause or there is consent by the party searched.

What Is a Search?

What is in plain view of whomever cares to look cannot be the subject of a search. This is true even if the things seen are in a place protected from physical intrusion.

A number of cases have involved viewing the openly visible contents of locked automobiles from the outside. This is not a search, even when done with the aid of a flashlight beam. In one case involvin a searchlight beam projected from one boat ontothe deck of another, the Supreme Court said that such viewing was not a search, and as such was the same as looking through binoculars.

Many decisions have held that surveillance through windows or other regular building apertures from the outside does not constitute a search. If the blinds are not drawn, the things within are not being kept private from whomever cares to observe them.

Harder cases are presented when keyholes or other openings not normally closed fro privacy are the means of observation. There is a strong tendency here to find that no search has occurred unless there was physical intrusion, in the case of seeing things as well as in the case of hearing them. But it is decided quite consistently that where the police have themselves made the opening for their observation, there is a physical intrusion and hence a search.

Perhaps the most delicate test to which these principles have been put is in the decision of a recent California case involving observation by an officer of the Long Beach Police Department at an amusement park in that city. A pipe extended through the roof above pay toilets, and when uncapped gave a view of two of the toilet booths to the officer on the room. A regular watch for long hours was maintained in the hope of apprehending persons engaged in criminal homosexual activity, and the dedication of the police officer was rewarded one night by a view of the anticipated infamous crime again nature. In finding that this constituted an unlawful search, the court pointed out that this was not a preliminary inspection by one about to make an arrest for which he already had probable cause; that it was a general exploratory search conducted solely to find evidence of guila, a practice condemned by both Federal and state law; and that an enclosed toilet booth, even though in a public toilet in a public amusement park, was a place of privacy for the occupant and entitled to the same protection as if it were in his home. The fact that the pipe was not installed by the police, and that the removal of its cap was outside the protected premises, made no difference.

Search with a Warrant

The authority for the legality of the search with a warrant is the Fourth Amendment to the Constitution, "and no warrants shall issue but upon probable cause . . ." The federal rules for determining legality of the warrant have been partially codified in Rule 41 of the Rules of Criminal Procedure, and the states have similar statutes. The rules governing the other types of legal searches have not been codified and are found in decisions of the courts.

Rule 41 which is solely applicable to federal courts, embodies the procedural requirements for obtaining a warrant. It must be based on a sworn statement from which the court can decide if there is reason to believe a crime has been committed and if the things to be seized have some relation to the crime. In setting up some standard for determining whether "probable cause" for the issuance of the warrant exists, the courts have said that it "means more than suspicion; there must be knowledge and information sufficient in themselves to warrant a man of reasonable caution to believe that an offense has been or is being committed." In other words, if you or I, as reasonably cautious people, know facts which justify us in thinking some crime has been or is being committed, the requirements of probable cause are satisfied.

The actual description of the premises may not be necessary so long as they are clearly indicated, for example, by giving the name of the occupant. A private dwelling may only be searched on such a warrant. A police officer who has to rely on the sworn statement of witnesses is protected, though the statements are actually untrue, if he has believed the statements and relied on them.

But there is nothing in the law which says anyone can obtain a blanket warrant for any property or papers of a person believed to be guilty of a crime. On the contrary, as we have seen, the article must be clearly connected with the commission of crime such as the gun with which it was committed, or the fruits of the crime such as the stolen articles, or the books used to record the transactions in question. If the property sought is merely evidence that the crime was committed as, for example, a letter to a friend making damaging admissions, a warrant cannot be obtained for its seizure. To seize it is to force the possessor to give evidence against himself in clear violation of the Fifth Amendment. A search warrant calling for the seizure of a stated item will not authorize the seizure of something else. However, in a recent federal case, where the warrant described counterfeiting apparatus, the courts held counterfeit stamps might be taken. Furthermore, partial illegality in the search does not vitiate the entire seizure and not every variation in the warrant will be deemed fatal.

In addition to the prohibitions in state constitutions against unreasonable search and seizure, all of the states have implemented this with criminal code provisions describing the issuance and execution of the search warrants. These sections detail the grounds upon which a warrant may be issued by a magistrate to a police officer, and nearly all the provisions, with some minor variations, read somewhat as follows: A warrant may be issued upon probable cause supported by affidavits when the property was used as a means of committing a felony or was stolen or embezzled, or when it is in the possession of a person who intends to use it to commit a public offense or when it is in the possession of another for concealment purposes. As in the case of the issuance of a federal warrant, the names and places must be shown to the magistrate. In addition, there are statutory provisions in the liquor laws, and in the Children's Court Act with which we are not concerned at present, detailing the procedure in special cases.

Use of Force in Connection with Search

Just as, in the case of the making of an arrest, an officer who used unnecessary force might create in the person arrested certain legal rights, so in the case of a search, the officer who exceeds his authority or uses unnecessary severity to serve his warrant may find himself liable for damages in a civil suit and will be subject to a fine or face sentence.

A citizen who honestly believes that a search is being conducted in violation of his constitutional rights would be wiser not to interfere with the search, but to give notice that he is not consenting to it. He may then seek damages from the officers and make a motion in the proper court for the return of the articles seized. The purpose of these remedies is to protect the rights of the individual and they serve to deter officials from arbitrary and unlawful acts. Both officers and private persons who procure warrants on false statements for malicious reasons are subject to a fine and one year imprisonment. There is also a penalty for searching without a warrant or "maliciously and without probable cause" searching any building or property, and the penalty is higher for a second offense than for a first. Here, too, the answer lies in the desire of the legislative branch to protect the individual from unwarranted invasions of his home and property. And though the statutes cited are federal, a check of the law of your state will reveal similar provisions.

. But, the federal government and some of the states also have statutes authorizing the breaking open of doors states have statutes authorizing the breaking open of doors or windows of a house or any part of the house to execute the search warrant if, after giving notice of his authority and purpose, the officer is refused admission.

He may also use like force when necessary to liberate himself or someone aiding him from the building. Congress has also seen fit to enact a statute providing that whoever impedes or obstructs the execution of a search warrant or a search and seizure being conducted in the line of duty shall be fined up to $5,000 or sentenced up to three years, or both. The penalty is even higher for using a deadly weapon to impede the course of such a search. There is also a penalty for destroying the property to be seized. The purpose of these statutory provisions is to protect the officer who is doing his duty.

Search without a Warrant

CIRCUMSTANCES JUSTIFYING DISPENSING WITH WARRANT; PROBABLE CAUSE: Since it is not always possible or practical to procure a search warrant, circumstances may dictate an immediate seizure to prevent the destruction of the property or its removal from the officer's jurisdiction. What then? The Constitution does not prevent all searches, only "unreasonable" ones. Prohibition and the problems of enforcement it created, led to the rule that it is not unreasonable to search without a warrant when the object to be searched is something movable such as a vehicle rather than a private dwelling. If the officer has "probable cause" to believe that the vehicle contains contraband, he may search it. Any other rule would make it impossible for the narcotics squad and the customs men to enforce the law. It is to be noted, then, that practical reasons form the basis for the exception made in the case of moving structures, not the wording of the Fourth Amendment, though the exception could be sustained on the ground that the amendment only refers to "house."

The same rationale was used to justify the search of a person going from an airplane into a bus. However, should the car be stored in a garage, so that there is ample time to procure a warrant, an officer would not be safe in relying on the "moving vehicle" exception. And if he wishes to search some place other than a private dwelling, even if he has probable cause for making the search, he would be taking a chance in assuming that no warrant is necessary. The federal courts have held that a business office is protected to the same extent as a home and may only be searched with a warrant, but that some outbuildings near a home, such as a barn, or open fields, are not.

A word of caution to those who must effect a search without a warrant! The manner of making the search may affect the validity of the seizure. The use of too much force may render the seizure bad. In one federal case, officers chased a car which they believed was being used to violate the law, and when close to it, fired at the tires. The court held the action improper and reversed a conviction based on evidence taken when the car was searched. Trickery, deceit or fraud practiced by the officer to effect the search will be viewed in the same manner as force, and may make the search and seizure "unreasonable." A curious twist to this, however, is that, if the force or trickery is used by someone who is not an officer to obtain the items, and he then turns them over to the officer, the person wronged has no redress because none of his constitutional rights was violated. (The Constitution protects only against governmental, not private action). Though this may seem to encourage snooping and tale-bearing on the part of neighbors, it is not always the function of the law to protect our privacy in every way.

SEARCH INCIDENT TO A LAWFUL ARREST: Innocuous as they seem, the words, "a search conducted as an incident of a lawful arrest is legal without a warrant,"

61

are fraught with hidden dangers. This is one of the well-known exceptions to the requirement of a warrant and reams have been written by textwriters and judges as to what is a lawful arrest, and still more as to what is meant by "incidental to" such an arrest. On the score of legality of arrest, no problems arise if it is made pursuant to a legally issued arrest warrant. However, when a search is made in connection with an arrest without an arrest warrant, the legality of the search and seizure in the first instance is dependent upon whether or not the arrest is one that could be made without a warrant in the state involved. But even if the arrest is legal, that does not necessarily mean that every seizure of goods connected with it is "reasonable."

Search of the person—There has never been any question about the right of an officer to search the person of someone legally arrested, and anything found on him may be validly seized which bears some relationship to the crimes for which he is being arrested. If it has no such relationship to the crime, but its possession is illegal, it may also be seized. The original theory behind this was that anything which may be used to commit further crime or to harm the officer, or which might be easily destroyed, or used to effect an escape, may be seized. The trend now goes beyond this and permits anything found on the person which is even evidence of a crime to be seized.

Cases in which bodily searches are an issue typically involve persons suspected of hiding narcotics, of drunken driving, of rape.

When there were facts justifying arrest based on suspicion of narcotics possession, a rectal examination by a physician under proper sanitary conditions was held not to be an unreasonable search.

Fluoroscopic examination of the stomach was followed by a laxative and then an emetic to recover narcotics previously swallowed, in another case. The person had not been arrested, but submitted to the procedure voluntarily after the dangers of leaving a packet of heroin in his stomach were explained to him. Again no violation of a Constitutional right was found in obtaining the narcotims under these circumstances.

Where a blood sample was taken by a physician from an unconscious accident victim to determine the likelihood of intoxication, the absence of consent under the circumstances did not make this search and seizure a violation of Constitutional rights. But where a police officer performed chemical tests to determine the presence of blood on the penis of an unwilling man who had been lawfully arrested and charged with rape, violation of his rights was found by the court. A similar determination has been made in more than one case where the person arrested was subjected to involuntary stomach pumping, though under proper medical conditions. The Supreme Court held in one such case that this procedure was so fundamentally objectionable that it was a denial of due process of law quite apart from being an unreasonable search and seizure.

A search of "the person" has been interpreted to mean a search of his clothing, the contents of his pockets, and things under his immediate control. These things, rather than bodily content, are the frequent subject of claims of unreasonable search of the person.

When a lawful arrest is made, search of the person is a lawful incident of it. Examination of clothing and its contents are clearly proper, but the question of what is under the immediate control of the person arrested is problematic. Coming to a man's home with a warrant for his arrest is not authorization to search his house. Yet the fact that he is not wearing his jacket when the arrest is made—it is lying on a chair nearby—does not exclude the jacket or its contents from a lawful search.

It is impossible to fix general rules for what is within the immediate control of a person arrested. Courts tend to find a greater range of immediate control when the place of arrest is public, or at least not the sort of place which is protected against unreasonable searches. This is logical since security of possessions require personal control over them in a public place, but not in a private place which is itself secure and so affords security for things within it. The problem is to avoid dissipating protection against unreasonable search of home or other protected place simply because an arrest is made there.

Search of things in the immediate control—But how far may an officer go in searching beyond the person of the arrestee? The same rules that apply to search of the person extend to search of his immediate personal effects such as handbags, trunks, and articles of clothing laid aside temporarily. The rule is stated in terms of permitting search of anything under his immediate control, and any articles found which are illegal may be seized. Here again, it would seem that what is merely evidence of another crime may not be the object of the search. If evidence of the commission of a felony is in plain sight, however, when the officer is making a legal arrest, he would be justified in arresting without a warrant for the commission of that felony, and hence may seize the visible evidence as an incident to the second arrest. But this is not the same thing as saying that he may actually search for evidence of another crime. Often, the case will resolve itself into a question of fact as to whether the officer was legitimately searching for something connected with the offense for which the arrest was being made or whether he was merely conducting a general exploratory search such as is frowned on by the law.

It has been held in some states, for example, that if the driver of a car is arrested for a minor traffic violation, anything which a search of the car turns up which serves to prove even another offense may be legally seized though it bears no relation to the offense for which the driver was arrested. A curious result—because there is no justification to search for anything on an arrest for violating traffic laws! However, to justify a search of the car which is not being conducted as an incident to an arrest, the officer must have "probable cause" such as would justify the issuance of a warrant, or he must suspect the presence of the illegal item. To render the seizure "reasonable," the article seized must be contraband and not merely evidentiary.

It is important to note that people are not protected only against search and seizure of property which they are legally entitled to possess. Things may be wrongfully in a person's possession — stolen goods, for instance—and the protection applies no less. It is invasion of privacy, not disturbance of property, which the law seeks to prevent. If showing that the property was stolen served to make lawful its earlier seizure, the police would enjoy the privilege of taking a calculated risk that a particular search might turn out to be reasonable, depending upon what it does or does not produce. What the Fourth Amendment seeks to prevent is police intrusion, mistaken or otherwise, unless such intrusion seems in advance to be reasonable under the circumstances. A search which may seem desirable to the police, even when weighed against the risks of finding nothing, may be very far from reasonable.

"Papers" include every sort of written thing, business and personal, corporate and individual. To come within the protection papers must belong to the person claiming it or be in his care. Either condition will suffice.

Public records, or papers of a sort in which the public has a legitimate interest, do not receive the same degree of protection for their privacy as do private papers. What may be be an unreasonable demand for inspection or an unreasonable examination with regard to private papers may be quite reasonable when the papers are affected with a public interest.

Search of the premises—If an arrest takes place off the premises, a search of the premises without a warrant is unreasonable. In a recent federal case, the officers, after observing certain premises for a time, arrested the occupants of a car seen leaving there and believed to be carrying illegal liquor after the car was already on a public road. The ensuing search of the premises for a still was held not to be incidental to the arrest, but a search of the persons of the occupants and of the car itself would be lawful.

Since the constitutional protection applies only to "house," a preliminary question for the courts is "what is a house?"

There is no real agreement among the various state courts as to whether buildings around the house are included in the protection as part of the premises, but they are generally agreed that garages are covered and open fields are not. The federal courts have also held that the dwelling need not be occupied at the time. In one interesting federal case, the officers procured an arrest warrant, but were instructed to hold off until the suspect entered the apartment before effecting the arrest. When he was ultimately arrested, a search of the apartment was declared not to be incidental to a lawful arrest because he should have been arrested earlier, and hence not reasonable.

But even where an arrest is properly made in a dwelling, the officers are not given carte blanche to ransack the entire house merely because the arrestee is in it. Again, any illegal objects that would tend to prove some crime other than that for which the arrest is being made, or instrumentalities or fruits of crime which are plainly visible may be seized—either under a federal foreiture statute or because the officer would be justified in arresting for the possession of these articles without a warrant since a felony is being committed in his presence.

But what if the objects are not visible but discovered after an extensive search of locked drawers and filing cabinets? Is this not the very right of privacy which the Constitution was designed to protect? There have been rapid developments in this phase of the law in recent years and the trend in the federal cases is toward allowing such searches. In a 1948 Supreme Court case, an arrest was made in one room but a search of the other rooms of a four-room apartment was made under a search warrant, and the seizure of property belonging to the United States and establishing another crime than that for which the warrant was issued, was declared lawful. And in another and slightly later Supreme Court case, the majority of the court permitted officers arresting with a warrant based on the forging of four "overprints" on cancelled stamps to search a one-room place of business for other forged stamps.

However, there are more recent lower court cases which still hold, and correctly so, that a general "fishing expedition" is not warranted. Where the officers, because of the nature of the crime for which they are arresting, cannot expect a search to reveal any fruits of the crime or instrumentalities, they may not actively search for evidence of its commission. For example, where the arrest was made on a warrant for harboring and concealing a fugitive from justice, though a search of defendant's person was lawful, a search of his letter files was not. Certainly the fugitive was not to be found hiding there. The papers found could only be used as evidence and were neither illegally in defendant's possession nor fruits or instrumentalities of crime, nor could they be used to effect his escape. In the absence of a showing that there was a specific object for which the search was started, or that there was probable cause to believe something was present which was illegally in defendant's possession such as stolen goods, the search could not be justified.

In these recent decisions, the Supreme Court seems to be making the character of the property a criterion in determining the validity of the seizures. Where O. P. A. gasoline ration stamps were seized at a place of business by officers acting without a warrant, though the decision was actually based on the fact that the defendant had consented, the court spoke approvingly of the right of officers to inspect public documents. And where draft cards were found after ransacking a person's home under a search warrant describing checks used in forgeries as the object, the conviction of the defendant for illegal possession of these cards was upheld, probably on the ground that they were government property. And in a case where title to the property was forfeit to the government under the Internal Revenue Laws, a seizure of property, seen at an earlier time on the premises, and seized without a search warrant, was approved on the ground that the United States had a right to the property. But where the property uncovered by the search does not belong to the United States or is not subject to forfeiture on sight, the officer who conducted the search may find himself guilty of exceeding his authority.

The term "houses" has been given broad interpretation in according protection.

Automobiles are protected places, though the standard for unreasonable search is quite different than in the case of a home. When a person drives his car on a public road, he is in a private, not a public, place and the car is protected from arbitrary inspections and seizures of its contents. The same holds true when the unoccupied car stands parked in a public place. Because of its mobility, however, suspicious circumstances may make inspection of a car reasonable without obtaining a warrant for this purpose, while under the same suspicious circumstances an on-the-spot search of a home, without warrant, would be unreasonable.

In New York, the protection has been held to extend to a taxicab while in the hire of the person claiming protection, and it is safe to state that not ownership, but temporary use and possession is the requisite for a claim of protection.

Offices, stores, factories, and other places of business are all within the Constitutional protection. Any place which is part of a person's place of business is included.

The same view is taken with regard to dwellings. Barns and garages, for instance, are generally recognized as part of the home. When the facts indicate they are not part of the home, they are excluded from protection. Open land is protected if it is part of the homestead. But unfenced or unbounded land which is not treated as part of one's home generally is not protected.

Hotel rooms, if used as a home even temporarily, are protected. The single-day transient guest, living out of his suitcase, has been denied protection for his room in some cases, and accorded it in others. If the circumstances indicate an affirmative answer to the question "did he in any sense live there while he occupied the room?" protection is in order. The crucial consideration is the existence of some right to exclude the rest of the world, even though short-lived.

Buildings need not be occupied to be protected. The

premises may be vacant. If they would be entitled to protection when occupied, they cannot be arbitrarily searched when unoccupied. The same reasoning applies conversely, so that places abandoned to the world may be freely searched.

Boats and ships are protected. Less stringent standards are applied to determine the reasonableness of the search, from the same consideration of mobility which applies to automobiles.

NECESSITY TO PROCURE A WARRANT: Closely related is the question of necessity to procure a warrant. In the moving vehicle cases, the explanation of the waiving of the warrant requirement was on the grounds that its procurement was impractical. However, this same line of Supreme Court cases stands for the proposition that time and opportunity to procure a warrant are not the controlling factors in determining the reasonableness of a search, though it is conceded that the requirement that one be procured may be appealing from the vantage point of easy administration.

> "Whether there was time," says Justice Minton speaking for the majority of the court, "may well be dependent upon considerations other than the ticking off of minutes or hours. The judgment of the officers as to when to close the trap on a criminal committing a crime in their presence or who they have reasonable cause to believe is committing a felony is not determined solely upon whether there was time to procure a search warrant. Some flexibility will be accorded law officers engaged in daily battle with criminals for whose restraint criminal laws are essential."

The doctrine of these cases comes dangerously close to an authorization of general searches. In Justice Frankfurter's famous answer to the arguments of the majority, which bids fair to earn for him a new crown as The Great Dissenter, the protection of the innocent was given as the reason the founding fathers subordinated police action to legal restraints.

"The knock at the door under the guise of a warrant of arrest for a venial or spurious offense was not unknown to them. . . . We have grim reminders in our day of their experience. Arrest under a warrant for a minor or a trumped-up charge has been familiar practice in the past, is a commonplace in the police state of today, and too well-known in this country. . . . The progress is too easy from police action unscrutinized by judicial authorization to the police state."

Consent

There is nothing in the law which protects a man against himself. In other words, if a person under suspicion wishes to cooperate with the law enforcement officials, and consents, either by his express words or by his actions, to an unreasonable search and seizure, he cannot, at some later date, invoke the protection of the Fourth Amendment. By giving consent, in the eyes of the law, he has waived his constitutional rights. However, the circumstances of a search are such that the suspect often "cooperates" in such a state of fear that in reality we have coercion or duress. And the courts, recognizing this obvious fact, have jealously protected the rights which he unwillingly surrendered. The consent must be freely and voluntarily given. In a case in which the person was placed under arrest before the search, they have been merciless in their scrutiny of the circumstances surrounding the search to determine whether his acts were induced by fear of superior numbers.

At this point, you have already decided that what you are about to read can have no application to you. You are not a Kentucky "hill billy" manufacturing your own corn liquor and ducking the "revenooers," nor are you a member of a sinister narcotics ring. But even you, Mr. Average Citizen, might be tempted to try to smuggle a piece of antique jewelry past the customs men on return from a trip abroad just for the heck of it. Or you might, even tomorrow, be the recipient of an innocent appearing visit from an agent of the Internal Revenue Bureau who wishes to check your books to see if you "forgot" to report some items of income in 1953. What is the effect of your saying, "Go right ahead boys. I have nothing to hide."? Or perhaps you were subpoenaed by a Grand Jury investigating a gambling syndicate and you, being a law-abiding citizen, produce the ticket stub and other proof to show how you won $10,000 on a horse. But you did not report your winnings on your income tax and at some later date you find yourself in a jam with the Collector of Internal Revenue. Can you procure the return of the evidence that you gave the Grand Jury and prevent its use or did you surrender it voluntarily?

In such instances, it rests with the government to establish the absence of duress, actual or implied. "Invitations" to enter a house when officers are armed and demand entrance have been held to have been secured by force. So too, when the officer displays his badge and declares that he has come to make a search, the reply of the occupant of the house that it is, "All right" has been held not to be a voluntary consent. The courts feel that consent, in such cases, was not "fully and intelligently given," and the plight of the defendant makes his consent explainable on the basis of physical or moral compulsion. However, in one case where an officer searching was a friend and former employee, failure to object to the search was considered an assent to it because fear was not involved.

In a recent federal case, a man appeared before a senate committee under compulsion of a subpoena. In the course of the questioning, he was repeatedly told his answers were likely to involve him in a citation for contempt or perjury. After constant threats of prosecution, on "request," he produced his books and records. The court examined all the testimony at the hearing and concluded that "his freedom of choice had been dissolved in a brooding omnipresence of compulsion." His production of private papers was consequently held to be an unreasonable seizure to which he had not consented.

In still another recent federal case, a taxpayer, on request, showed an internal revenue agent his books and papers. The agent later brought in another agent who was in the criminal division, but failed to notify the taxpayer of this fact and warn him that he might stand on his constitutional rights. Both agents returned at a time when no one was present and opened cabinets containing material that the taxpayer had never shown to the agent. The court pointed out that consent had been given under a misunderstanding of the true facts and that failure to apprise the defendant of the fact that criminal proceedings were contemplated and that he could stand on his constitutional rights negated the consent. Then, too, the agents had availed themselves of materials not voluntarily given. The distinction may appear to be finely drawn, but the fact remains that one cannot consent to what one does not know. Consent given to an examination for civil purposes cannot be converted to a search for criminal purposes.

There is some indication that if the Treasury Department's policy not to prosecute those who make voluntary disclosures is used as a ruse to induce the giving of incriminating evidence for which the government intends to prosecute, the taxpayer will be held not to have consented voluntarily to the disclosures. It is significant that not every failure to warn the defendant of his constitutional rights will be considered material on the issue of consent, and not every failure on the part of a defendant to claim his constitutional rights will constitute a waiver of them.

When the evidence is obtained from third parties to whom the defendant voluntarily released it rather than from the defendant, constitutional rights are held not to be violated. When a party goes into bankrupty, he has been held to have voluntarily given up his papers so that they may be taken from the receivers having custody without violating the constitution. And when the defendant had voluntarily filed papers with a federal court or administrative agency in some prior action or hearing and they are obtained from that court or agency, or where the disputed papers were obtained by state officers acting entirely on their own efforts and not aided or instigated by federal officers, or were filed as a public record, there is no violation of constitutional rights. In all of these examples, the defendant voluntarily surrendered the papers to the third party from whom they were obtained and can no longer claim the constitutional protection. Consent to a search can be given by an agent. An office manager or a superintendent of an apartment house will be considered an agent and may give consent in the place of the owner of the property. While it has not been decided whether a wife can consent for her husband, it has been held that a mother-in-law cannot.

Search by Postal Authorities and Department of Health Officers

Though interception of sealed matter in the mail is protected by the Fourth Amendment, federal postal inspectors are granted rights by Act of Congress to search for mailable matter transported in violation of the law. On authorization from the Postmaster General, they may search any vehicle which has lately passed through the post office or any common carrier transporting such matter or any warehouse in which it is stored. They may not, however, examine such matter in a private dwelling because the opening of a mailed item, unless specifically permitted by statute, is a violation of the Fourth Amendment. Prison authorities also have authority, by virtue of their position, to open and inspect letters and packages of prisoners.

In many localities, health officials are given authority to inspect private dwellings without obtaining a warrant. In 1949, the Supreme Court had an opportunity to decide whether a search of a home by such an official, in the absence of a compelling emergency, violated the Fourth Amendment, but avoided doing so. There is, however, some lower court authority indicating that, in the absence of a warrant, such a search is unreasonable.

Who Is Protected?

A search may violate the rights of more than one person—the owner of an article and the one in whose care he has left it, for example. If, however, a person simply has possession, without any sort of interest in the thing—a messenger boy, for instance—it is obvious that a search and seizure

73

will not be an invasion of his privacy, and so not a violation of his Constitutional right. Of course such a person may still have a claim of unlawful search or seizure of his person, if the situation included such acts.

A person may have a firm and fundamental legal interest in property, and yet not be entitled to claim Constitutional protection. A landlord normally would not be able to assert the illegality of a search and seizure of an apartment or office which was leased. The tenant's privacy, but not the landlord's, was violated. The same result was reached where a husband had legal title to a house occupied by his estranged wife. The fact that he did not live there at all was what mattered. And where a group or association is so impersonal in its scope of membership and activities that it is not simply an extension of the private interests of its members, the right of individual members to be secure against unreasonable searches is not violated by a search of the group's papers.

The circumstances alone may import the privacy of one person into the property of another. Thus, although a wife had no legal interest in a house owned by her husband, a search of it was a violation of her privacy because of the relation of husband and wife. But a husband does not have a right of privacy with regard to his wife's body, at least not the sort which is violated by unreasonable searches. Only the wife may claim Constitutional protection in this case.

An employee has a right of privacy at his place of employment. In one instance the employee's desk was searched by the police with the employer's permission. The court found that since the desk was given over to the employee for his exclusive use, the right to be free from searches was his to give up or insist upon, as he chose, and not his employer's.

Only the person whose privacy has been violated may claim the protection. The fact that the wrongful consequences affect another person does not confer Constitutional rights on that other person. Thus, if there is an unlawful search of one man's house and evidence of a crime committed by another man is obtained, the other man cannot avail himself of Constitutional remedies by claiming that the evidence is the product of a violation of Fourth Amendment guaranties and must be suppressed. And the owner of the house, unless he is implicated in the crime, has no standing to demand such suppression.

It is important to recognize that the Constitutional guaranty against unreasonable search applies to persons who have criminal records and are notorious as professional criminals in the same way that it applies to everyone else. Numerous times courts have held that the suspect's criminal notoriety does not make a search more reasonable. The independent probability that a time has been committed, which may be indicated by various circumstances, is what is to be considered. The proven penchant for crime of the suspect is not a proper circumstance for such consideration. Although the police frequently find such niceties burdensome, our legal system cherishes a distinction between rights to be accorded one who does not stand convicted, and one who does.

Corporations are entitled to the protection of the Fourth Amendment. The concept of privacy for corporate affairs is somewhat different than for individuals, and intrusions into corporate privacy is considered more reasonable in many instances. The corporation is a creature of the state, and public authority which has created it reserves the right, to some extent, to look into its affairs. Particularly is this true when the corporation's business is largely a matter of public concern—public utilities being the extreme case.

All persons within the jurisdiction of the United States, aliens and citizens alike, are entitled to protection under the Fourth Amendment.

Remedies of Owner or Possessor of Illegally Seized Property

Redress may exist in one of several forms—an action for damages against an officer making the seizure, a civil action to compel return of the property seized, or a motion made before trial to compel the return of the property and to suppress its use as evidence. The right to compel return is a purely personal one and if the property came into the state's hands via a third party, or if the defendant has no right of possession, this remedy is unavailable. The same is true of a defendant's right to raise the constitutional question in the federal courts to prevent use of the seized matter in evidence.

The remedies open to the defendant in any jurisdiction which holds that the seized property may be used as evidence on a criminal trial are very unsatisfactory. The loss of his job by an officer is of slight consolation to the wronged party. In the federal courts, however, the defendant is protected first by the federal rule of evidence which prohibits the use of this evidence against him, on the grounds that the Fifth Amendment is involved, and second, by the procedure set up in Rule 41(e) of the Rules of Criminal Procedure. Under this rule he may move the District Court before trial for return of the property and to suppress its use as evidence. If the motion is granted, the property must be returned unless otherwise subject to lawful detention and is inadmissible in evidence. The motion must be made before the introduction of the evidence in any trial is sought and the judge will not rule on this collateral issue during a trial. However, if the defendant, for one of a variety of good reasons, was unable to make the special motion, such as not knowing the government possessed the evidence until it was offered on the trial, the judge may in his discretion hear argument on the issue at any time. However, the defendant in a state court is not entitled to the benefit of these rules by virtue of the Fourteenth Amendment because they are rules of evidence and not substance.

Admissibility of Evidence Acquired by Illegal Search and Seizure

A landmark verdict (1959) in criminal law was handed down by the U. S. Supreme Court when it ruled that evidence seized by state officials in violation of the federal constitution cannot be introduced in a federal trial. In overturning the so-called "silver platter" doctrine, the high court upheld the claim that admission of such evidence would violate the right of privacy guaranteed by the Fourth Amendment. The majority opinion was based on the reasoning that to let federal courts utilize illegally obtained state evidence was "to encourage subterfuge by federal law enforcement officials."

A year later, the Supreme Judicial Court of Massachusetts acquitted a Smith College instructor for possession of obscene pictures and literature because the evidence against him had been seized in an illegal search of his apartment. The decision represented a direct application on the state level of the Supreme Court holding.

The effect of judicial fiat has been to render applicable in all of the states a rule that legislatively had applied in some 20 states, to the effect that *evidence illegally obtained by search and seizure is inadmissible.*

The arguments for and against the exclusionary rule may be summarized as follows: On the one side is the serious need to repress crime; on the other, the equally serious requirement that law shall not be flouted by officers sworn to uphold it. Or, put somewhat differently, is it better to let a few criminals escape justice than to injure society by condoning enforcement of the law by flouting the law? The Supreme Court appears to have settled the argument in behalf of rejecting illegality as a method of repressing crime.

Right to Privacy of One's Telephone and Telegraph Communications

FEDERAL LAW OF WIRE TAPPING: Who doesn't vaguely remember something about the inability to convict a suspected traitor because the evidence against her was inadmissible. And within the past few years, the newspapers have been regaling us with stories of the vain attempts of the Attorney General to get Congress to pass a bill legalizing wiretaps. What is it all about?

In 1937, the Supreme Court held that the Federal Communications Act of 1934 applied to the disclosure of facts in court which had been learned by listening in to telephone conversations. This Act prohibits anyone who receives or assists in receiving messages from publishing or delivering them to anyone but the addressee. It must have come as a shock to agents enforcing the laws of the United States to learn that this Act prohibited them from either introducing recordings or telephone conversations in court or of testifying as to the contents of those to which they had listened. There is nothing to indicate that Congress, when passing the Communications Act, either intended or foresaw the uses to which it would be put. This is a bit of judicial legislation in which the policy was to protect the privacy of the individual at the expense of law enforcement. And the inability of the present Attorney General to secure passage of a bill legalizing wire tapping is a strong indication that the lawmakers still favor such a policy.

THE LAW IN THE STATES: Although the Federal Communications Act has been held to apply to both interstate and intrastate conversations it is not binding on the states and many have enacted their own legislation. Some provide that physical tampering with the wires such as cutting or injuring or interfering with communication constitute a misdemeanor. Punishment results only from actual interference with transmission. By far the greatest number of states have provisions aimed specifically at wire tapping. Some states have more than one statute, the enactment of the latter evidencing the increased concern over intangible rights in need of protection. Other states penalize not only the wire tapping but also the divulgence. Testimony arising out of wire tapped conversations is not necessarily excluded in Arizona, California, North Dakota, Montana, Oklahoma, because disclosure is allowed on the obtaining of a court order. In New York, a warrant may be procured by certain officials authorizing the wiretapping. In Louisiana, Oklahoma and Massachusetts, public officers are not included in the prohibition against wire tapping. In fact, there is a question, as yet unsettled, whether they are included in many of the state statutes.

Some states, among them Delaware, New Jersey and

Rhode Island forbid, by statute, testifying to wire-tapped information. And in a few other states including California, Maryland, Massachusetts, Minnesota and New York, the courts have arrived at the same result without benefit of statute. Most of the others do not appear to follow the federal rule in denying admissibility to information procured in violation of the wire-tap statutes. In the few cases in point, the state courts have been guided by the letter of the statutes rather than the spirit. Expressing regret at being unable to decide otherwise, they have been strict in their interpretations of the specific statutes, and if the defendant's act was not a violation of the express language, they have refused to convict.

Five states—Maryland, Massachusetts, New York, Nevada and Oregon—permit court-approved wiretapping by law enforcement officials, thereby carving out a specific exception to the general enforcement of wiretapping legislation. But in any case, evidence gained from wiretapping, although illegal, would not necessarily be excluded by operation of the Supreme Court rule mentioned above (see p.   ), since that rule is applicable to evidence obtained in violation of the Constitution. Apparently, evidence obtained in violation of federal and/or state laws is not similarly proscribed, and wiretapping itself does not fall in the category of an unlawful search and seizure in violation of constitutional prohibitions.

To summarize, evidence obtained by wiretap is excluded in federal courts by operation of federal legislation. In the states, the picture is not so clearcut. In general, evidence illegally obtained by other than a law enforcement officer will not be admitted; but evidence illegally obtained by a law enforcement officer may be admitted.

EVIDENCE INDIRECTLY OBTAINED THROUGH WIRETAP: It was all very well for the U.S. Supreme Court to rule that evidence directly obtained by wiretaps might not be introduced, but what if it was indirectly obtained? It has been held that such evidence is also inadmissible. The question as to whether evidence was indirectly obtained can be raised by a defendant on a preliminary motion. He then has the burden of proof to show that his wires were tapped, but once he has shown it, the government may have to show that it did not make use of anything overheard. If confessions can be shown to have been obtained after playing recordings of conversations in which the confessor participated, they will not be admissible because indirectly procured by disclosure of the telephone communications. Even if both parties to the conversation confess, it cannot be considered equivalent to a consent to its use because the consent is not voluntarily given. However, if the parties to the incriminating convercation confess on the basis of the recordings and their testimony is used against fellow conspirators, the latter cannot be heard to object to the indirect use to obtain the confessions. They were not parties to the conversations and are therefore not protected by the Communications Act from a divulging of the contents. It is qualifications like this which make it difficult for an enforcement officer to apply the law. Such a qualification as the instant one is undoubtedly based on the language of the statute and not on any policy considerations.

As the federal law stands today, one party to a conversation may not consent to its divulgence by testifying to the conversation in court. However, a federal agent or any one else being in the room while a telephone conversation is in progress, can testify to what he heard, unless he is listening in on an extension. To eavesdrop on one end of a conversation involves no interception of any message. It has also been held that police officers who raided defendant's apartment and picked up the phone when it rang could testify to the ensuing conversation one had with the party on the other end who believed he was talking to the defendant. The accused was held not to be a "sender" of the message and hence not entitled to the protection of the Act.

USE OF DEVICES NOT INVOLVING WIRE-TAP: Nor does the use of a detectaphone placed against the wall in an adjoining apartment which enables the agent to hear defendant speaking on the phone constitute a violation of the Act. No "interception" of wire communication is involved. This was also held not to be such an invasion of privacy as to violate the Fourth Amendment. Congress obviously did not intend to cut off all resort by federal agents to trickery, spying, posing and eavesdropping in the detection of crime. The wiretapping legislation was only intended to protect against the most insidious form of secret eavesdropping, namely, the listening in on calls of which both parties are ignorant.

It has also been held that where an informer entices a suspect into a conversation, wearing a device under his coat which picks up the conversation and transmits it to an agent outside the premises, neither the Fourth Amendment nor the Communications Act is violated. Where the officers of the State of California were guilty of the most flagrant violation of the rights of an individual, it was held not to be such an invasion of privacy as is prohibited by the Constitution. They had committed a trespass by entering defendant's home in his absence. Holes were bored in his roof through which wires were run into a neighboring garage for a microphone. Still later they concealed the microphone in his bedroom closet. The defendant strenuously objected to the admissibility of the evidence thus produced on the grounds that both the Federal Communications Act and the Fourth Amendment were violated. In holding that the evidence was admissible, the Supreme Court reiterated the fact that admissibility of evidence is a procedural matter and peculiarly within the province of the state, hence the Fourth and Fourteenth Amendments had no application. Nor was the Federal Communications Act violated. Discussing the policy which leads to exclusion of the evidence, the court said, "Rejection of the evidence does nothing to punish the wrongdoing official, while it may, and likely will, release the wrongdoing defendant. It deprives society of its remedy against one lawbreaker because he has been pursued by another. It protects one against whom incriminating evidence is discovered but does nothing to protect innocent persons who are the victims of the illegal and fruitless searches."

Right to be Secure Against Unreasonable Orders to Procure Books and Papers, Subpoena Duces Tecum

In this era of government by administrative agencies and law enforcement by congressional and senatorial committees, it is not unusual for the most law-abiding citizen to find himself served with a subpoena to produce his books and records. This is known as a subpoena duces tecum and is the process also used to compel production of records in civil suits. A party has no grounds for objecting to the subpoena in a civil case unless it is too broad in its coverage or unless the infomation to be divulged is of a criminal nature because his opponent is, by the Constitution itself, granted the right to compel the testimony of witnesses. However, where the records are sought by a grand jury or in a criminal trial, or by a legislative or administrative investigatory body, he may find that one of his constitutional rights is being impinged upon, either the privilege to be secure against unreasonable search and seizure or the privilege against self-incrimination.

THE FIFTH AMENDMENT. It follows that the proposition that a man cannot be forced to give incriminating testimony against himself which is found in both state and federal constitutional provisions should also apply to the forced production of any books or records that would incriminate him or subject him to some criminal charge. His production of the records is a voucher of their genuineness, and hence testimony. The protection of the Fifth Amendment or the state constitutional provision extends equally to demands to produce made before there is any accusation of a crime as well as after indictment. There is no need to go into the moral depravity which would ensue were a system of justice to prevail which permits the extraction from a suspect of evidence against himself. Although analysis of the history, philosophy and constitutional bases for the privilege will appear in this work when we are discussing the rights of the accused at the time of his trial, we are as yet concerned only with his rights at the time of the arrest, search for evidence, and preliminary procedures for investigation prior to prosecution.

Since in this era of industrialization, many businesses are incorpated, it should be made clear at the onset that anything hereafter said about the privilege against self-incrimination does not apply to orders to produce corporate books and records. Nor are the officers of the corporation protected if any matters found in such records would serve to incriminate them. The privilege also does not apply to records required to be kept by law such as druggists' reports or pawnbrokers' records of sales, or to a record made by a public official in the course of his duties since it is open to inspection by the public at any time. If the subpoena is directed, not to the person incriminated but to a third person, the privilege, being a personal one, cannot be claimed. For this reason, a defendant who filed papers in a bankruptcy proceeding cannot successfully object to an order directed to the receiver or custodian to produce them.

If, by act of the legislature, the grant of a right to issue a subpoena is coupled with a grant of immunity to the person compelled to produce documents, he has no further grounds to contest the subpoena. If he cannot, by the very words of the statute, be prosecuted for anything which his records may reveal, how can be claim he is being com pelled to give evidence which will incriminate him?

THE FOURTH AMENDMENT: As a general proposition, it has been held that the service of a legally issued subpoena to produce books and records does not constitute an unreasonable search and seizure. Of course, the subpoena must have been issued by a legislative or judicial body which has ben granted the subpoena power by some legislative act, and all of the requirements of that act must have been complied with. Private persons, protected by the privilege against self-incrimination, have no need to seek the added protection of the Fourth Amendment, but corporations which are not so protected, have frequently endeavored to invoke it. What little help it affords them is based on the requirement that the disclosure sought shall not be unreasonable.

The requirements of reasonableness have been spelled out by the courts. It is not necessary, as in the case of issuance of a warrant, that a charge or complaint be pending as long as the investigation is within the power of Congress to make. This ruling often appears in relation to grand jury investigation or general or statistical investigations authorized by the legislature. As in the case of issuance of the warrant, there is a requirement of "probable cause" supported by oath or affirmation, but this is satisfied if the court finds the investigation one within the power of Congress to initiate, and if the documents sought are relevant to the inquiry. Whereas, in the case of a warrant, the place to be searched and persons or things to be seized must be particularized, here the requirement is only that the documents to be produced be adequately specified. However, this does not mean that every document sought must be described along with the purpose for which it is sought, though the subpoena may not be so broad and indefinite as to approach in character a general warrant or writ of assistance, nor may it allow a search through all papers, "relevant or irrelevant in the hope that something will turn up." There can be no set formula given for determining the exact measure of specificity required, for the nature and breadth of the subpoena must of necessity vary with the nature, purpose and scope of the injury. It will suffice to state that some subpoena may be found to be "unreasonable" because too general.

A situation may arise which will be held to amount to a constructive search, as where officers arresting corporate officials at home, made an illegal search of the company offices, seized papers, had them copied, and after being forced by court order to return the originals, then served subpoenas to compel the production of the original papers. The government, in such a case, cannot use the subpoena as a subterfuge to avoid the effects of its initial wrong. However, where records were subpoenaed for a grand jury which was subsequently dismissed because it was improperly impanelled, the United States Supreme Court dismissed a motion to compel their return and prevent their use in evidence on the grounds that this did not amount to a seizure in violation of the Fourth Amendment.

85

GLOSSARY

ARREST. The apprehending of a person to answer charges of a crime.

CONSENT. A free and voluntary waiver of constitutional rights under the Fourth Amendment.

ENTRAPMENT. The implanting by government agents of the intention to commit a crime in the mind of an otherwise innocent person.

EXCLUSIONARY RULE. A 60 year old Supreme Court rule, based on the Fourth, Fifth, and Sixth Amendments, that requires courts to exclude from the courtroom all illegally seized evidence. Also known as the SUPPRESSION RULE.

FRISK. A search or a limited patting of the outer surfaces of a person's clothing in an attempt to find weapons.

POISONOUS FRUIT DOCTRINE. Evidence that is initially obtained unconstitutionally becomes the "poisonous tree." When the (primary) illegally-obtained evidence leads to other evidence, then this other (secondary) evidence becomes the "fruit of the poisonous tree."

PRIVILEGE. The legal protection from disclosure of certain confidential socially important relationships, such as husband and wife, attorney and client, physician and patient and the President and his advisors.

PROBABLE CAUSE. Facts or apparent facts, viewed through the eyes of the law enforcement officer, that generate a reasonable belief that someone is about to commit or has committed a crime.

RIGHT TO COUNSEL. A Sixth Amendment right of an accused to have an attorney represent him "at every critical stage" of a criminal proceeding.

RIGHT TO PRIVACY. A Fourth Amendment right of every citizen to be left alone by the government unless there are facts or probable cause to justify searches or seizures against him.

RIGHT AGAINST SELF-INCRIMINATION. A Fifth Amendment right of an accused to not be compelled by the government to testify against himself or produce personal papers or documents that might tend to incriminate him.

SEARCH. Looking into or prying into places for the purpose of finding incriminating evidence.

SUPPRESSION HEARING. A pretrial criminal evidentiary hearing, held before a judge sitting without a jury, to determine whether the incriminating evidence obtained by the prosecution was obtained lawfully.

CRIME CLASSIFICATIONS

The following are brief definitions of the crime classifications utilized in the national Uniform Crime Reporting program.

1. **Criminal homicide.** (a) Murder and nonnegligent manslaughter: all willful felonious homicides as distinguished from deaths caused by negligence. Excludes attempts to kill, assaults to kill, suicides, accidental deaths, or justifiable homicides. Justifiable homicides are limited to: (1) the killing of a person by a peace officer in line of duty; (2) the killing of a person in the act of committing a felony by a private citizen. (b) Manslaughter by negligence: any death which the police investigation establishes was primarily attributable to gross negligence of some individual other than the victim.

2. **Forcible rape.** Rape by force, assault to rape and attempted rape. Excludes statutory offenses (no force used — victim under age of consent).

3. **Robbery.** Stealing or taking anything of value from the care, custody, or control of a person by force or violence or by putting in fear, such as strong-arm robbery, stickups, armed robbery, assaults to rob, and attempts to rob.

4. **Aggravated assault.** Assault with intent to kill or for the purpose of inflicting severe bodily injury by shooting, cutting, stabbing, maiming, poisoning, scalding, or by the use of acids, explosives, or other means. Includes attempts. Excludes simple assault, assault and battery, fighting, etc.

5. **Burglary.** Breaking or entering — Burglary, housebreaking, safe-cracking, or any breaking or unlawful entry of a structure with the intent to commit a felony or a theft. Includes attempts.

6. **Larceny.** Theft (except auto theft) (a) Fifty dollars and over in value; (b) under $50 in value. Thefts of bicycles, automobile accessories, shoplifting, pocket-picking, or any stealing of property or article of value which is not taken by force and violence or by fraud. Excludes embezzlement, "con" games, forgery, worthless checks, etc.

7. **Auto theft.** Stealing or driving away and abandoning a motor vehicle. Excludes taking for temporary use by those having lawful access to the vehicle.

8. **Other assaults.** Assaults and attempted assaults which are not of an aggravated nature.

9. **Arson.** Willful or malicious burning with or without intent to defraud. Includes attempts.

10. **Forgery and counterfeiting.** Making, altering, uttering or possessing, with intent to defraud, anything false which is made to appear true. Includes attempts.

11. **Fraud.** Fraudulent conversion and obtaining money or property by false pretenses. Includes bad checks except forgeries and counterfeiting.

12. **Embezzlement.** Misappropriation or misapplication of money or property entrusted to one's care, custody, or control.

13. **Stolen property; buying, receiving, possessing.** Buying, receiving, and possessing stolen property and attempts.

14. **Vandalism.** Willful or malicious destruction, injury, disfigurement, or defacement of property without consent of the owner or person having custody or control.

15. **Weapons; carrying, possessing, etc.** All violations of regulations or statutes controlling the carrying, using, possessing, furnishing, and manufacturing of deadly weapons or silencers. Includes attempts.

16. **Prostitution and commercialized vice.** Sex offenses of a commercialized nature and attempts, such as prostitution, keeping a bawdy house, procuring or transporting women for immoral purposes.

17. **Sex offenses (except forcible rape, prostitution, and commercialized vice).** Statutory rape, offenses against chastity, common decency, morals, and the like. Includes attempts.

18. **Narcotic drug laws.** Offenses relating to narcotic drugs, such as unlawful possession, sale, use, growing, manufacturing, and making of narcotic drugs.

19. **Gambling.** Promoting, permitting or engaging in gambling.

20. **Offenses against the family and children.** Nonsupport, neglect, desertion, or abuse of family and children.

21. **Driving under the influence.** Driving or operating any motor vehicle or common carrier while drunk or under the influence of liquor or narcotics.

22. **Liquor laws.** State or local liquor law violations, except "drunkenness" (class 23) and "driving under the influence" (class 21). Excludes Federal violations.

23. **Drunkenness.** Drunkenness or intoxication.

24. **Disorderly conduct.** Breach of the peace.

25. **Vagrancy.** Vagabondage, begging, loitering, etc.

26. **All other offenses.** All violations of state or local laws, except classes 1-25 and traffic.

27. **Suspicion.** Arrests for no specific offense and released without formal charges being placed.

28. **Curfew and loitering laws (juveniles).** Offenses relating to violation of local curfew or loitering ordinances where such laws exist.

29. **Runaway (juveniles).** Limited to juveniles taken into protective custody under provisions of local statutes as runaways.

GOVERNMENT OF THE DISTRICT OF COLUMBIA
Metropolitan Police Department

December 1, 1971

GENERAL ORDER No. 602–1

SUBJECT: Automobile Searches and Inventories

The purpose of this order is to establish the policy and procedures governing searches and inventories of vehicles. This order consists of the following part:

PART I Responsibilities and Procedures for Members of the Department

Part I

A. *Searches.*

A search is an examination of a person, place or thing with a view toward discovery of weapons, contraband, instrumentalities of a crime, or evidence. It is to be distinguished from an inventory. A search of an automobile can be classified in one of the following categories:

Searches connected with an arrest.

Searches not connected with an arrest.

1. *Searches Connected With an Arrest.*

a. *No Probable Cause to Believe Evidence Is in the Vehicle.*

(1) *General Rule.*

If a full custody arrest is made of a subject in a motor vehicle and the officer does *not* have probable cause to believe that the vehicle contains fruits, instrumentalities, contraband, or evidence of the crime for which he has been arrested, only those areas which are within the immediate control of the defendant (the area from which the arrested person might gain possession of weapons or destructible evidence) at the time of his arrest may be searched incident to that arrest. The search shall be conducted in the presence of the defendant. (The scope, time and place of the search shall be governed by part I, paragraphs A1a(2) and A1a(3) of this order.)

Examples of searches with no probable cause are:

(a) *Carrying a Dangerous Weapon.* An officer making a routine traffic stop observes a pistol in the glove compartment which was opened by the driver

91

as he reached for his automobile registration. The driver is arrested for carrying a dangerous weapon. Only those areas of the interior of the vehicle within the driver's immediate control at the time of his arrest should be searched because there is no probable cause to believe there is other evidence of the offense for which he was arrested in the vehicle.

(b) *Full Custody Traffic Arrest.* An officer arrests a driver of a vehicle for driving after revocation. Before he is transported to a district station, those areas of the vehicle within the immediate control of the defendant at the time of his arrest should be searched, However, areas beyond his immediate control should not be searched because there is no cause to believe that the vehicle contains fruits, instrumentalities, contraband, or evidence of the offense of driving after revocation.

(2) *Scope of the Search.*

The arresting officer may search all areas of the vehicle which are within the *immediate control* of the defendant at the time of his arrest, including those areas from which he might gain possession of a weapon or destructible evidence. If items discovered during his limited search give the officer probable cause to believe that fruits, instrumentalities, contraband, or other evidence of a crime is in the vehicle, then those areas of the vehicle which could physically contain such evidence shall be searched. An example of the scope of the search is:

An officer arrests a driver of a vehicle for driving after revocation. A search under the driver's seat, incident to the arrest, reveals a bottlecap cooker and syringe. The officer may now search the entire vehicle since there is probable cause to believe that other implements of a crime may be in areas of the vehicle beyond the immediate control of the defendant.

(3) *Time and Place of the Search.*

If a full custody arrest is made of a subject in or near a vehicle and the officer does not have probable cause to believe that fruits, instrumentalities, contraband, or evidence of the crime for which the arrest was made may be found in that vehicle, the limited search of that vehicle incident to the arrest shall be conducted at the time and place of the arrest within the immediate presence of the defendant.

92

(4) *Plain and Open View Rule.*

Nothing in this order should be construed to limit the authority of an officer to seize any item which he observes in plain and open view (including items observed in plain view at night by means of a flashlight) beyond the immediate control of a subject, if the officer has probable cause to believe that such item constitutes fruits, contraband, instrumentalities, or evidence of a crime.

(5) *Non-Custodial Arrests.*

Traffic violators who are asked to accompany an officer to a district station (e.g., non-resident traffic violators who commit moving violations) and are not placed under full custody arrest shall not be searched and their vehicles shall not be searched unless an officer reasonably suspects the violator to be armed, in which case the subject may be frisked for weapons.

b. *Probable Cause to Believe Evidence Is in Vehicle.*

(1) *General Rule.*

If a full custody arrest is made of a subject in a motor vehicle or of a subject in close proximity to a motor vehicle who has just departed from or is about to enter a vehicle, and the arresting officer has probable cause to believe that the vehicle contains either fruits (e.g., stolen goods), instrumentalities (e.g., tools used in a burglary), contraband (e.g., narcotics, sawed-off shotgun), or evidence (e.g., clothing worn by a robber) of the crime for which he was arrested, the vehicle shall be searched. (The scope, time and place of the search shall be governed by part I, paragraphs A1b(2) and A1b(3) of this order.) Examples of probable cause searches are:

(a) *Vehicle Used in Robbery.* An officer has observed a vehicle described in a lookout for a robbery holdup which occurred one hour earlier, in which two men wearing ski masks and carrying pistols obtained an undetermined amount of money. After arresting the two occupants of the vehicle, the entire vehicle should be searched at the scene of the arrest since the officer has probable cause to believe that the money obtained and the pistols and ski masks used in the robbery may be hidden in areas within and beyond the immediate control of the suspects.

(b) *Sales of Narcotics from Vehicle.* A plainclothes officer arrests a subject in or near a vehicle. He has

93

had the subject under observation for the previous hour for the sale, from the vehicle, of narcotics to individuals who approached the vehicle. All areas of the vehicle should be searched since the officer has probable cause to believe that a supply of narcotics remains in other areas of the vehicle, such as the trunk or glove compartment.

(2) *Scope of the Search.*

When an officer arrests a subject in or near a vehicle and he has probable cause to believe that vehicle contains fruits, instrumentalities, contraband, or evidence of the crime for which the arrest was made, only those areas of the vehicle which could physically contain that evidence shall be searched. Examples of the scope of the search are:

(a) *Vehicle Used in Burglary.* An officer has stopped a vehicle for a traffic spot check and has been informed by the dispatcher that the vehicle has been reported as being used in a burglary which occurred a few hours earlier in which a portable television set was stolen. Since it is generally known that most burglaries are effected by means of small tools, easily concealed, all areas of the vehicle may be searched for such tools, unless the officer has specific information that entry was gained in a manner other than by use of a small tool. In such a case, only those areas of the vehicle which could physically contain the portable television set or the object used to enter the premises may be searched because they are the only areas for which the officer has probable cause to believe that fruits, instrumentalities, or evidence of the crime for which the arrest has been made may be contained.

(b) *Vehicle Containing Large Object Used in a Homicide.* A vehicle is stopped, pursuant to a lookout, for a suspect wanted in connection with a homicide in which the deceased was struck with a tire iron which the assailant was seen carrying toward the vehicle. The officer should not search the locked glove compartment because the large object could not be contained in such a small space. The trunk, however, should be searched for the object. If, however, there is some other missing item of evidence (e.g., a blood-stained glove of the suspect), the locked glove compartment may be searched if there is probable cause

94

to believe that the item is in the possession of the suspect or in the vehicle at the time of the arrest.

(3) *Time and Place of Search.*

The search of the vehicle shall be conducted as soon as the prisoner is placed in secure custody and ordinarily at the scene of the arrest. It is not necessary to keep the prisoner near the vehicle during this type of search. In those exceptional cases where it is not practical to conduct a search of the automobile at the scene of the arrest, the vehicle shall be removed to a police facility or other area where the search shall be conducted as soon as possible. In those cases where the search is conducted at a place other than the scene of the arrest, an officer shall remain with the vehicle to ensure a continuous chain of custody prior to the search. Examples of exceptional cases where search may be delayed are:

(a) *Keys to Locked Area not Available.* When the search of a locked trunk or glove compartment of a vehicle is not possible at the scene of the arrest because keys are not available, the officer shall notify the Auto Theft Section and request that a set of keys be sent to the location to which the vehicle has been taken. If the keys are not available, instructions shall be obtained from the Property Division as to the method to be used in opening the locked trunk or glove compartment. No search warrant is required, but the search shall be conducted as soon as possible.

(b) *Hostile Crowd or Inclement Weather.* When an officer believes it would be advisable to remove a vehicle from a public location prior to searching it because a hostile crowd has formed or because the weather is inclement, the vehicle may be taken to the nearest police facility and searched promptly without a warrant.

(1) *Search Warrant.*

When an officer arrests a subject in or near a vehicle and he has probable cause to believe that the vehicle contains fruits, instrumentalities, contraband, or evidence of the crime for which the subject is arrested, all those areas of the automobile which can contain such evidence shall be searched *without* a search warrant. In those exceptional cases where the search is not completed at the scene of the arrest and the vehicle is removed to a police facility or other

95

area, the search shall be completed, as soon as possible, *without* a search warrant. In cases where there is adequate time to obtain a search warrant *prior* to the arrest of a subject in a vehicle, a warrant shall be obtained for the search of the vehicle. One example of the necessity for a search warrant is:

Adequate Time to Obtain Search Warrant Before Making Arrest in Vehicle. A subject has been under surveillance for several days because of the officer's suspicion that he is selling stolen property from his vehicle. If probable cause to arrest is gathered and the decision is made to obtain an arrest warrant for the subject, a search warrant for the vehicle should also be obtained because there is adequate time to do so.

2. *Searches Not Connected with an Arrest.*

General Rule. If an officer has probable cause to believe that a parked, unoccupied vehicle, whether locked or unlocked, contains fruits, instrumentalities, contraband, or evidence of a crime, all those areas of the vehicle which can contain such evidence shall be searched without a search warrant if the vehicle appears to be in such operational condition that it can be moved or easily rendered movable by minor repairs. If, however, a vehicle does not appear to be movable and there is adequate time in which to obtain a search warrant, such warrant shall be obtained prior to entering the vehicle. One example of such a search is:

An officer has been informed by a citizen that he observed a person place a sawed-off shotgun in the trunk of a vehicle one-half hour earlier. The citizen gives his name and address and accompanies the officer to the vehicle, which appears to be operational except for a flat rear tire. The officer may immediately search the trunk of the vehicle without a search warrant because he has probable cause to believe that the shotgun is in the trunk of the vehicle and the vehicle may be easily rendered movable by a minor repair. If, however, the vehicle has been completely stripped, including the wheels, the officer should obtain a search warrant prior to searching the trunk of the vehicle.

B. *Inventories.*

An inventory is an administrative process by which items of property are listed and secured. An inventory is not to be considered or used as a substitute for a search. Automobiles coming into the custody of the police department shall be classified for purposes of this paragraph relating to inventories in one of the following five categories:

Seizures for purposes of forfeiture.

Seizures as evidence.

Prisoner's property.

Traffic impoundments.

Non-criminal impoundments.

The officer's right to inventory an automobile and the time and scope of any such inventory depend upon the category into which it is classified.

1. *Seizures for Purposes of Forfeiture.*

    a. *Narcotics.* When an officer has probable cause to believe that a vehicle has been used to transport illegally possessed narcotics, he shall take the vehicle into custody and classify it as a seizure for purpose of forfeiture *only if both of the following conditions exist*:

        (1) A substantial amount of drugs is involved.

        (2) The owner of the vehicle (not necessarily the user of the vehicle) is a significant drug violator.

No seizure under this paragraph shall be made without approval of an official of the Narcotics Branch. If a vehicle used to transport illegally possessed narcotics cannot be seized under this paragraph, it may not be inventoried unless it can be classified and inventoried under another section of part I, paragraph B of this order. An example of seizures based on narcotics violations is:

An officer stops an automobile and observes a glassine envelope containing a small amount of a substance which he has reason to believe is heroin in plain and open view of the floor boards. The driver (who is the owner of the vehicle) is arrested for illegal possession of narcotics. The officer contacts an official of the Narcotics Branch and is informed that because the driver has no previous narcotics record and the amount of narcotics seized is not substantial, the vehicle may not be seized for purposes of forfeiture. It may be classified, however, as prisoner's property pursuant to part I, paragraph B3 of this order and inventoried to the extent allowed under the rules contained in that paragraph.

    b. *Gambling.* When an officer has probable cause to believe that a vehicle is being or has been used to conduct illegal gambling activities, it may be seized for purposes of forfeiture, irrespective of the age, value, or condition of the vehicle.

        (1) *Authorization.* No seizure under this paragraph shall be made without approval of an official of the Gambling and Liquor Branch.

        (2) *Examples of Seizures for Purposes of Forfeiture*

Based Upon Gambling Violations.

(a) *Vehicle Used by Numbers Runner.* After surveillance, officers develop probable cause to believe that a person is a numbers runner and that a vehicle which he owns or used has been used to conduct the numbers operation. The officers obtained an arrest warrant and a search warrant for his vehicle. When the officers execute the arrest warrant during one of the runs, the defendant's vehicle may be seized for purposes of forfeiture if such seizure has been approved by an official of the Gambling and Liquor Branch.

(b) *Arrest for Possession of a Numbers Slip.* On a routine traffic stop an officer observes in the driver's wallet a single numbers slip and arrests the driver for its possession. If the evidence indicates that the driver was simply a person who placed a numbers bet rather than one who was involved in *conducting* a gambling operation, the vehicle may not be seized for purposes of forfeiture.

c. *National Firearms Act Violations.* When an officer has probable cause to believe that a vehicle has been used to transport a firearm possessed illegally under the National Firearms Act (49 U.S.C. SS 781–788), he shall follow the procedures contained in General Order No. 601.1 in determining whether the vehicle shall be seized for purposes of forfeiture under the Act.

d. *Procedure.* An officer who seizes an automobile for purposes of forfeiture shall completely inventory the contents of the automobile immediately upon its arrival at a police facility. The scope of that inventory shall be limited by the rules provided in part I, paragraph B6 of this order. Upon completion of the inventory, the officer shall obtain instructions from an official of either the Narcotic or Gambling and Liquor Branch or from an agent of the Alcohol, Tobacco and Firearms Division of the Internal Revenue Service, relating to appropriate further processing of the vehicle.

2. *Seizures as Evidence.*

When an officer has probable cause to believe that a vehicle is a fruit, instrumentality, or evidence of a crime, he shall take the vehicle into police custody and shall classify it as a seizure as evidence.

a. *Examples of Seizures as Evidence.*

(1) *Homicide in an Automobile.* A citizen is shot to death in an automobile. After appropriate on-the-scene processing by the Homicide Section, the vehicle shall be seized as evidence because it is evidence and, in addition, may contain evidence of the offense.

(2) *Vehicle Used in an Offense.* Two days after a bank robbery an officer locates an automobile which has been described by witnesses as the getaway vehicle. Whether or not an arrest has been made in the case, the vehicle shall be seized as evidence because it is an instrumentality of the offense of bank robbery.

NOTE: Although whenever there is either a moving or a parking traffic violation the vehicle involved is technically evidence of that offense, vehicles shall *not* be seized as evidence simply because they were involved in relatively minor traffic offenses. However, if a vehicle has some evidentiary value beyond the fact that it was used to commit a minor traffic offense it shall be seized as evidence.

b. *Procedure.* An officer who seizes a vehicle as evidence shall completely inventory the contents of the vehicle immediately upon its arrival at a police facility, provided that such an inventory will not damage or destroy any evidence contained therein. The scope of that inventory shall be limited by the rules provided in part I, paragraph B6 of this order.

c. *Release of Vehicle.* Vehicles seized as evidence shall not be released to any person until the appropriate prosecutor has signed the proper release form indicating that the vehicle is no longer needed as evidence. In cases where a prosecutor is unavailable and application of this rule would result in hardship to an innocent party, verbal authorization may be obtained by telephone from an Assistant United States Attorney on emergency duty for the month or from any other available Assistant United States Attorney.

3. *Prisoner's Property.*

When a person is arrested in an automobile which he owns or has been authorized to use and the vehicle cannot be classified under part I, paragraph B1 or B2 of this order, that vehicle shall be classified as prisoner's property. One example of prisoner's property is:

Robbery Suspect. A liquor store owner has been robbed by a single assailant who fled on foot. Ten days after the offense the defendant is arrested on a warrant in an automobile. Since there is no basis for seizing the automobile either as evidence or for purposes of forfeiture, the auto-

mobile shall be classified as prisoner's property.

a. *Disposition of Prisoner's Property.* A vehicle which is classified as prisoner's property shall be disposed of in any lawful manner in which the person arrested directs. In any case where a prisoner requests that his vehicle be lawfully parked on a public street, he shall be required to indicate his request in writing. An example of disposition of prisoner's property is:

Robbery Arrest. In the robbery example above, the defendant is accompanied by his wife at the time of his arrest. If the defendant so requests, his wife shall be permitted to drive the vehicle from the scene of the arrest. If the defendant is alone at the time of arrest and requests that the vehicle be lawfully parked pending notification of his wife, the request shall be honored, so long as he indicates his request that the vehicle be so parked in writing.

b. *Initial Procedure.* If a vehicle classified as prisoner's property is disposed of so that it is not taken to a police facility, it shall not be inventoried in any way. If it is necessary to take such a vehicle into police custody, the vehicle shall be taken to a police facility or to a location in front of or near a police facility. Immediately upon arrival at the police facility the arresting officer shall remove from the passenger compartment of the vehicle any personal property which can easily be seen from outside the vehicle and which reasonably has a value in excess of $ .5. After removing such property, if any, the officer shall make sure that the windows are rolled up and the oors and trunk are locked. Any property so removed sh. be brought into the police facility and appropriate enuics and returns made in accordance with General Order No. 601.1. No other inventory or search of the vehicle shall be made at this time.

c. *Procedure After 24 Hours.* If a person authorized by the prisoner or the prisoner himself, upon his release, does not claim the vehicle within 24 hours of the time that the prisoner was arrested, a complete inventory of the contents of the automobile shall be made by the arresting officer or an officer designated by an official. The scope of that inventory shall be limited by the rules provided in part I, paragraph B6 of this order.

4. *Traffic Impoundments.*

Only those vehicles which, pursuant to section 91 of the D.C. Traffic and Motor Vehicle Regulations, are taken into police

custody *and* placed on police department property or at a location in front of or near a police facility shall be classified as "traffic impoundments." Vehicles classified as traffic impoundments shall be inventoried *only* in accordance with part I, paragraphs B4d and B4e of this order. If a vehicle is not placed on police department property or near a police facility, it is not a traffic impoundment and shall not be inventoried or searched in any way.

   a. *Non-Impounded Vehicles.* Except as provided in part I, paragraph B4c below, whenever an officer causes a vehicle to be moved pursuant to the traffic regulations, the vehicle shall, if possible, be moved to a location on a public street as close to the original location as possible, consistent with prevailing traffic conditions.

   b. *Procedure in Non-Impoundment Situations.* Vehicles moved but not taken to a police facility or to a location in front of or near a police facility shall not be classified as traffic impoundments and shall not be inventoried or searched in any way. However, the officer who caused the automobile to be moved shall make sure that the windows of the automobile are rolled up and, if possible, the trunk and doors are locked before he leaves the vehicle. In all cases where a vehicle is moved without the knowledge of the owner, the Teletype Branch shall be notified in accordance with General Order No. 601.1. An example of a non-impoundment situation is:

   Illegal Parking on Main Arteries During Rush Hour. Illegally parked vehicles are disrupting the flow of traffic on a main artery during rush hour. The vehicles should be moved to a location as close to the original location as possible, consistent with prevailing traffic conditions. The vehicle shall not be inventoried or searched in any way.

   c. *Impoundments in Exceptional Circumstances.* Only in exceptional circumstances shall the vehicle be impounded for traffic violations and taken to police property or to a location in front of or near a police facility. Examples of exceptional circumstances are:

   (1) *Large Amounts of Personal Property in Plain View Within the Automobile.* A vehicle is unlawfully parked on Constitution Avenue during rush hour. Large amounts of clothing and a number of suitcases are in plain view on the back seat of the automobile. In order to protect the citizen's property, the automobile shall be impounded and towed to a police facility or to a location in front of or near a police facility.

(2) *Outstanding Traffic Warrants.* A vehicle is unlawfully parked in front of a fire hydrant. A WALES check discloses that there is a traffic arrest warrant outstanding for the registered owner in addition to 10 unpaid tickets. The vehicle shall be impounded and taken to a police facility or to a location in front of or near the police facility. The vehicle shall not be released to the citizen until collateral in the appropriate amount for the outstanding and present violations is posted.

In these circumstances, the vehicle may also be immobilized by use of a boot or other immobilizing device. If a vehicle is immobilized, rather than impounded and brought to a police facility, the vehicle shall not be inventoried in any way.

d. *Procedure in Impoundment Situations Upon Arrival at Police Facility.* Immediately upon arrival at the police facility, the impounding officer shall remove from the passenger compartment of the vehicle any personal property which can easily be seen from outside the vehicle and which reasonably has a value in excess of $25. After removing such property, if any, the officer shall make sure that the windows are rolled up and, if possible, that the doors and trunk are locked. Any property so removed shall be brought into the police facility and appropriate entries and returns made in accordance with General Order No. 601.1. No other inventory or search of the vehicle shall be made at this time. An example of an impoundment situation upon arrival at a police facility is:

Large Amounts of Personal Property in Plain View Within the Automobile. In the example above relating to large amounts of clothing and suitcases within the automobile, the officer shall remove the clothing and suitcases from the automobile *immediately* upon arrival at the police facility. He shall not examine the glove compartment, search under the seat, or make any other search at this time. The windows shall then be rolled up and the vehicle locked. Appropriate entries and returns shall be made in accordance with General Order No. 601.1.

e. *Procedure in Impoundment Situations After 24 Hours.* If a vehicle which has been impounded is not claimed by the registered owner or a person authorized by the registered owner with 24 hours of the time that the vehicle was impounded, a complete inventory of the contents of the automobile shall be made by the impounding officer or an officer designated by an official. The scope of that inventory shall be limited by the rules provided in part I, paragraph B6 of this order.

5. *Non-Criminal Impoundments.*

When an officer has taken a vehicle into police custody because there is reason to believe that it is abandoned, part of the estate of a deceased person, property of an insane person or a person taken to the hospital, or property turned over to the police at the scene of a fire or disaster, he shall classify it as a non-criminal impoundment.

Procedure. Since the vehicle may be in police custody for an undetermined period of time, an officer who impounds a vehicle as a non-criminal impoundment shall completely inventory the vehicle immediately upon its arrival at a police facility. The scope of that inventory shall be limited by the rules provided in part I, paragraph B6 of this order.

6. *Scope of Inventory.*

Whenever an officer has a right to inventory a vehicle pursuant to this order, the officer shall examine the passenger compartment, whether or not locked, and the trunk, whether or not locked. Any items of personal property which reasonably have a value in excess of $25 shall be removed from the vehicle and placed in secure custody. All items so removed shall be listed and recorded on a property return as provided in General Order No. 601.1. Any container such as boxes or suitcases found within the vehicle shall be opened and any items of personal property found in such containers which reasonably has a value in excess of $25 shall be listed and recorded separately. Immediately upon completion of the inventory, the officer shall make sure that the windows are rolled up and the doors and the trunk are locked.

(signed) *Jerry V. Wilson*
Chief of Police

Appendix C

The following is excerpted from Chief Justice Warren's opinion in *Miranda v. Arizona* (384 U.S. 436, 1965). The excerpt is significant for its statement of police methods of interrogation, and its analysis of such methods in the context of psychological as well as physical pressure applied to a suspect. So that the reader may appreciate the full scope of the decision, the headnotes are likewise reproduced. (Footnotes are excluded.)

OCTOBER TERM, 1965

Syllabus.

MIRANDA *v.* ARIZONA.

CERTIORARI TO THE
SUPREME COURT OF ARIZONA.

No. 759. Argued February 28—March 1, 1966.— Decided June 13, 1966.*

In each of these cases the defendant while in police custody was questioned by police officers, detectives, or a prosecuting attorney in a room in which he was cut off from the outside world. None of the defendants was given a full and effective warning of his rights at the outset of the interrogation process. In all four cases the questioning elicited oral admissions. and in three of them signed statements as well, which were admitted at their trials. All defendants were convicted and all convictions, except in No. 584, were affirmed on appeal. *Held:*

1. The prosecution may not use statements, whether exculpatory or inculpatory, stemming from questioning initiated by law enforcement officers after a person has been taken into custody or otherwise deprived of his freedom of

action in any significant way, unless it demonstrates the use of procedural safeguards effective to secure the Fifth Amendment's privilege against self-incrimination. Pp. 444-491.

(a) The atmosphere and environment of incommunicado interrogation as it exists today is inherently intimidating and works to undermine the privilege against self-incrimination. Unless adequate preventive measures are taken to dispel the compulsion inherent in custodial surroundings, no statement obtained from the defendant can truly be the product of his free choice. Pp. 445-458.

(b) The privilege against self-incrimination, which has had a long and expansive historical development, is the essential mainstay of our adversary system and guarantees to the individual the "right to remain silent unless he chooses to speak in the unfettered exercise of his own will," during a period of custodial interrogation as well as in the courts or during the course of other official investigations. Pp. 458-465.

(c) The decision in *Escobedo* v. *Illinois,* 378 U. S. 478, stressed the need for protective devices to make the process of police interrogation conform to the dictates of the privilege. Pp. 465-466.

(d) In the absence of other effective measures the following procedures to safeguard the Fifth Amendment privilege must be observed: The person in custody must, prior to interrogation, be clearly informed that he has the right to remain silent, and that anything he says will be used against him in court; he must be clearly informed that he has the right to consult with a lawyer and to have the lawyer with him during interrogation, and that, if he is indigent, a lawyer will be appointed to represent him. Pp. 467-473.

(e) If the individual indicates, prior to or during questioning, that he wishes to remain silent, the interrogation must cease; if he states that he wants an attorney, the questioning must cease until an attorney is present. Pp. 473-474.

(f) Where an interrogation is conducted without the presence of an attorney and a statement is taken, a heavy burden rests on the Government to demonstrate that the defendant knowingly and intelligently waived his right to counsel. P. 475.

(g) Where the individual answers some questions during in-custody interrogation he has not waived his privilege and may invoke his right to remain silent thereafter. Pp. 475-476.

(h) The warnings required and the waiver needed are, in the absence of a fully effective equivalent, prerequisites to the admissibility of any statement, inculpatory or exculpatory, made by a defendant. Pp. 476-477.

2. The limitations on the interrogation process required for the protection of the individual's constitutional rights should not cause an undue interference with a proper system of law enforcement, as demonstrated by the procedures of the FBI and the safeguards afforded in other jurisdictions. Pp. 479-491.

3. In each of these cases the statements were obtained under circumstances that did not meet constitutional standards for protection of the privilege against self-incrimination. Pp. 491-499.

98 Ariz. 18, 401 P. 2d 721; 15 N. Y. 2d 970, 207 N. E. 2d 527; 16 N. Y. 2d 614, 209 N. E. 2d 110; 342 F. 2d 684, reversed; 62 Cal. 2d 571, 400 P. 2d 97, affirmed.

. . . .

Opinion of the Court

MR. CHIEF JUSTICE WARREN delivered the opinion of the Court.

The cases before us raise questions which go to the roots of our concepts of American criminal jurisprudence: the restraints society must observe consistent with the Federal Constitution in prosecuting individuals for crime. More specifically, we deal with the admissibility of statements obtained from an individual who is subjected to custodial police interrogation and the necessity for procedures which assure that the individual is accorded his privilege under the Fifth Amendment to the Constitution not to be compelled to incriminate himself.

We dealt with certain phases of this problem recently in *Escobedo* v. *Illinois,* 378 U. S. 478 (1964). There, as in the four cases before us, law enforcement officials took the defendant into custody and interrogated him in a police station for the purpose of obtaining a confession. The police did not effectively advise him of his right to remain silent or of his right to consult with his attorney. Rather, they confronted him with an alleged accomplice who accused him of having perpetrated a murder. When the defendant denied the accusation and said "I didn't shoot Manuel, you did it," they handcuffed him and took him to an interrogation room. There, while handcuffed and standing, he was questioned for four hours until he confessed. During his interrogation, the police denied his request to speak to his attorney, and they prevented his retained attorney, who had come to the police station, from consulting with him. At his trial, the State, over his objection, introduced the confession against him. We held that the statements thus made were consitutionally inadmissible.

. . . .

We start here, as we did in *Escobedo,* with the premise that our holding is not an innovation in our jurisprudence, but is an application of principles long recognized and applied in other settings. We have undertaken a thorough re-examination of the *Escobedo* decision and the principles it announced, and we reaffirm it. That case was but an explication of basic rights that are enshrined in our Constitution—that "No person . . . shall be compelled in any criminal case to be a witness against himself," and that "the accused shall . . . have the Assistance of Counsel"—rights which were put in jeopardy in that case through official overbearing. These precious rights were fixed in our Constitution only after centuries of persecution and struggle. And in the words of Chief Justice

Marshall, they were secured "for ages to come, and . . . designed to approach immortality as nearly as human institutions can approach it," *Cohens* v. *Virginia,* 6 Wheat. 264, 387 (1821).

.   .   .   .   ,

Our holding will be spelled out with some specificity in the pages which follow but briefly stated it is this: the prosecution may not use statements, whether exculpatory or inculpatory, stemming from custodial interrogation of the defendant unless it demonstrates the use of procedural safeguards effective to secure the privilege against self-incrimination. By custodial interrogation, we mean questioning initiated by law enforcement officers after a person has been taken into custody or otherwise deprived of his freedom of action in any significant way. As for the procedural safeguards to be employed, unless other fully effective means are devised to inform accused persons of their right of silence and to assure a continuous opportunity to exercise it, the following measures are required. Prior to any questioning, the person must be warned that he has a right to remain silent, that any statement he does make may be used as evidence against him, and that he has a right to the presence of an attorney, either retained or appointed. The defendant may waive effectuation of these rights, provided the waiver is made voluntarily, knowingly and intelligently. If, however, he indicates in any manner and at any stage of the process that he wishes to consult with an attorney before speaking there can be no questioning. Likewise, if the individual is alone and indicates in any manner that he does not wish to be interrogated, the police may not question him. The mere fact that he may have answered some qustions or volunteered some statements on his own does not deprive him of the right to refrain from answering any further inquiries until he has consulted with an attorney and thereafter consents to be questioned.

I.

The constitutional issue we decide in each of these cases is the admissibility of statements obtained from a defendant questioned while in custody and deprived of his freedom of action. In each, the defendant was questioned by police officers, detectives, or a prosecuting attorney in a room in which he was cut off from the outside world. In none of these cases was the defendant given a full and effective warning of his rights at the outset of the interrogation process. In all the cases, the questioning elicited oral admissions, and in three of them, signed statements as well which were admitted at their trials. They all thus share salient features—incommunicado interrogation of individuals in a police-dominated atmosphere, resulting in self-incriminating statements without full warnings of constitutional rights.

An understanding of the nature and setting of this in-custody interrogation is essential to our decisions today. The difficulty in depicting what transpires at such interrogations stems from the fact that in this country they have largely taken place incommunicado. From extensive factual studies undertaken in the early 1930's, including the famous Wickersham Report to Congress by a Presidential Commission, it is clear that police violence and the "third degree" flourished at that time. In a series of cases decided by this Court long after these studies, the police resorted to physical brutality—beating, hanging, whipping—and to sustained and protracted questioning incommunicado in order to extort confessions. The 1961 Commission on Civil Rights found much evidence to indicate that "some policemen still resort to physical force to obtain confessions," 1961 Comm'n on Civil Rights Rep., Justice, pt. 5, 17. The use of physical brutality and violence is not, unfortunately, relegated to the past or to any part of the country. Only recently in Kings County, New York, the police brutally beat, kicked and placed lighted cigarette butts on the back of a potential witness under interrogation for the purpose of securing a statement incriminating a third party. *People* v. *Portelli*, 15 N. Y. 2d 235, 205 N.E. 2d 857 , 257 N. Y. S. 2d 931 (1965).

The examples given above are undoubtedly the exception now, but they are sufficiently widespread to be the object of concern. Unless a proper limitation upon custodial interrogation is achieved—such as these decisions will advance—there can be no assurance that practices of this nature will be eradicated in the foreseeable future . . . .

Again we stress that the modern practice of in-custody interrogation is psychologically rather than physically oriented. As we have stated before, "Since *Chambers* v. *Florida,* 309 U. S. 227, this Court has recognized that coercion can be mental as well as physical, and that the blood of the accused is not the only hallmark of an unconstitutional inquisition." *Blackburn* v. *Alabama,* 361 U.S. 199, 206 (1960). Interrogation still takes place in privacy. Privacy results in secrecy and this in turn results in a gap in our knowledge as to what in fact goes on in the interrogation rooms. A valuable source of information about present police practices, however, may be found in various police manuals and texts which document procedures employed with success in the past, and which recommend various other effective tactics. These texts are used by law enforcement agencies themselves as guides. It should be noted that these texts professedly present the most enlightened and effective means presently used to obtain statements through custodial interrogation. By considering these texts and other data, it is possible to describe procedures observed and noted around the country.

The officers are told by the manuals that the "principal psychological factor contributing to a successful interrogation is *privacy*—being alone with the person under interrogation." The efficacy of this tactic has been explained as follows:

"If at all practicable, the interrogation should take place in the investigator's office or at least in a room of his own choice. The subject should be deprived of every psychological advantage. In his own home he may be confident, indignant, or recalcitrant. He is more keenly aware of his rights and more reluctant to tell of his indiscretions or criminal behavior within the walls of his home. Moreover his family and other friends are nearby, their presence lending moral support. In his own office,

110

the investigator possesses all the advantages. The atmosphere suggests the invincibility of the forces of the law."

To highlight the isolation and unfamiliar surroundings, the manuals instruct the police to display an air of confidence in the suspect's guilt and from outward appearance to maintain only an interest in confirming certain details. The guilt of the subject is to be posited as a fact. The interrogator should direct his comments toward the reasons why the subject committed the act, rather than to court failure by asking the subject whether he did it. Like other men, perhaps the subject has had a bad family life, had an unhappy childhood, had too much to drink, had an unrequited attraction to women. The officers are instructed to minimize the moral seriousness of the offense, to cast blame on the victim or on society. These tactics are designed to put the subject in a psychological state where his story is but an elaboration of what the police purport to know already—that he is guilty. Explanations to the contrary are dismissed and discouraged.

The texts thus stress that the major qualities an interrogator should possess are patience and perseverance. One writer describes the efficacy of these characteristics in this manner:

"In the preceding paragraphs emphasis has been placed on kindness and stratagems. The investigator will, however, encounter many situations where the sheer weight of his personality will be the deciding factor. Where emotional appeals and tricks are employed to no avail, he must rely on an oppressive atmosphere of dogged persistence. He must interrogate steadily and without relent, leaving the subject no prospect of surcease. He must dominate his subject and overwhelm him with his inexorable will to obtain the truth. He should interrogate for a spell of several hours pausing only for the subject's necessities in acknowledgment of the need to avoid a charge of duress that can be technically substantiated. In a serious case, the interrogation may continue for days, with the required intervals for food and sleep, but with no respite from the atmosphere of domination. It is possible

111

in this way to induce the subject to talk without resorting to duress or coercion. The method should be used only when the guilt of the subject appears highly probable."

The manuals suggest that the suspect be offered legal excuses for his actions in order to obtain an initial admission of guilt. Where there is a suspected revenge-killing, for example, the interrogator may say:

"Joe, you probably didn't go out looking for this fellow with the purpose of shooting him. My guess is, however, that you expected something from him and that's why you carried a gun—for your own protection. You knew him for what he was, no good. Then when you met him he probably started using foul, abusive language and he gave some indication that he was about to pull a gun on you, and that's when you had to act to save your own life. That's about it, isn't it, Joe?"

Having then obtained the admission of shooting, the interrogator is advised to refer to circumstantial evidence which negates the self-defense explanation. This should enable him to secure the entire story. One text notes that "Even if he fails to do so, the inconsistency between the subject's original denial of the shooting and his present admission of at least doing the shooting will serve to deprive him of a self-defense 'out' at the time of trial."

When the techniques described above prove unavailing, the texts recommend they be alternated with a show of some hostility. One ploy often used has been termed the "friendly-unfriendly" or the "Mutt and Jeff" act:

". . . In this technique, two agents are employed. Mutt, the relentless investigator, who knows the subject is guilty and is not going to waste any time. He's sent a dozen men away for this crime and he's going to send the subject away for the full term. Jeff, on the other hand, is obviously a kindhearted man. He has a family himself. He has a brother who was involved in a little scrape like this. He disapproves of Mutt and his tactics and will arrange to get him off the case if the subject will cooperate.

He can't hold Mutt off for very long. The subject would be wise to make a quick decision. The technique is applied by having both investigators present while Mutt acts out his role. Jeff may stand by quietly and demur at some of Mutt's tactics. When Jeff makes his plea for cooperation, Mutt is not present in the room."

The interrogators sometimes are instructed to induce a confession out of trickery. The technique here is quite effective in crimes which require identification or which run in series. In the identification situation, the interrogator may take a break in his questioning to place the subject among a group of men in a line-up. "The witness or complainant (previously coached, if necessary) studies the line-up and confidently points out the subject as the guilty party." Then the questioning resumes "as though there were now no doubt about the guilt of the subject." A variation on this technique is called the "reverse line-up":

"The accused is placed in a line-up, but this time he is identified by several fictitious witnesses or victims who associated him with different offenses. It is expected that the subject will become desperate and confess to the offense under investigation in order to escape from the false accusations."

The manuals also contain instructions for police on how to handle the individual who refuses to discuss the matter entirely, or who asks for an attorney or relatives. The examiner is to concede him the right to remain silent. "This usually has a very undermining effect. First of all, he is disappointed in his expectation of an unfavorable reaction on the part of the interrogator. Secondly, a concession of this right to remain silent impresses the subject with the apparent fairness of his interrogator." After this psychological conditioning, however, the officer is told to point out the incriminating significance of the suspect's refusal to talk:

"Joe, you have a right to remain silent. That's your privilege and I'm the last person in the world who'll try to take it away from you. If that's the way you want to leave this, O.K. But let me ask you this. Suppose you were in my shoes and I were in yours and you called me in to ask me about this and I told you, 'I don't want to answer any of your questions.' You'd think I had something to hide, and you'd probably be right in thinking that. That's exactly what I'll have to think about you, and so will everybody else. So let's sit here and talk this whole thing over."

Few will persist in their initial refusal to talk, it is said, if this monologue is employed correctly.

In the event that the subject wishes to speak to a relative or an attorney, the following advice is tendered:

"The interrogator should respond by suggesting that the subject first tell the truth to the interrogator himself rather than get anyone else involved in the matter. If the request is for an attorney, the interrogator may suggest that the subject save himself or his family the expense of any such professional service, particularly if he is innocent of the offense under investigation. The interrogator may also add, 'Joe, I'm only looking for the truth, and if you're telling the truth, that's it. You can handle this by yourself.'"

From these representative samples of interrogation techniques, the setting prescribed by the manuals and observed in practice becomes clear. In essence, it is this: To be alone with the subject is essential to prevent distraction and to deprive him of any outside support. The aura of confidence in his guilt undermines his will to resist. He merely confirms the preconceived story the police seek to have him describe. Patience and persistence, at times relentless questioning, are employed. To obtain a confession, the interrogator must "patiently maneuver himself or his quarry into a position from which the desired objective may be attained." When normal procedures fail to produce the needed result, the police may resort to deceptive stratagems such as giving false legal advice. It is important to keep the subject off balance, for example, by trading on his insecurity about himself or his surroundings.

114

The police then persuade, trick, or cajole him out of exercising his constitutional rights.

Even without employing brutality, the "third degree" or the specific stratagems described above, the very fact of custodial interrogation exacts a heavy toll on individual liberty and trades on the weakness of individuals. This fact may be illustrated simply by referring to three confession cases decided by this Court in the Term immediately preceding our *Escobedo* decision. In *Townsend* v. *Sain,* 372 U. S. 293 (1963), the defendant was a 19-year-old heroin addict, described as a "near mental defective," *id.,* at 307-310. The defendant in *Lynumn* v. *Illinois,* 372 U. S. 528 (1963), was a woman who confessed to the arresting officer after being importuned to "cooperate" in order to prevent her children from being taken by relief authorities. This Court similarly reversed the conviction of a defendant in *Haynes* v. *Washington,* 373 U. S. 503 (1963), whose persistent request during his interrogation was to phone his wife or attorney. In other settings, these individuals might have exercised their constitutional rights. In the incommunicado police-dominated atmosphere, they succumbed.

In the cases before us today, given this background, we concern ourselves primarily with this interrogation atmosphere and the evils it can bring. In No. 759, *Miranda* v. *Arizona,* the police arrested the defendant and took him to a special interrogation room where they secured a confession. In No. 760, *Vignera* v. *New York,* the defendant made oral admissions to the police after interrogation in the afternoon, and then signed an inculpatory statement upon being questioned by an assistant district attorney later the same evening. In No. 761, *Westover* v. *United States,* the defendant was handed over to the Federal Bureau of Investigation by local authorities after they had detained and interrogated him for a lengthy period, both at night and the following morning. After some two hours of questioning, the federal officers had obtained signed statements from the defendant. Lastly, in No. 584, *California* v. *Stewart,* the local police held the defendant five days in the station and interrogated him on nine separate occasions before they secured his inculpatory statement.

In these cases, we might not find the defendants' statements to have been involuntary in traditional terms. Our concern for adequate safeguards to protect precious Fifth Amendment rights is, of course, not lessened in the slightest. In each of the cases, the defendant was thrust into an unfamiliar atmosphere and run through menacing police interrogation procedures. The potentiality for compulsion is forcefully apparent, for example, in *Miranda,* where the indigent Mexican defendant was a seriously disturbed individual with pronounced sexual fantasies, and in *Stewart,* in which the defendant was an indigent Los Angeles Negro who had dropped out of school in the sixth grade. To be sure, the records do not evince overt physical coercion or patented psychological ploys. The fact remains that in none of these cases did the officers undertake to afford appropriate safeguards at the outset of the interrogation to insure that the statements were truly the product of free choice.

It is obvious that such an interrogation environment is created for no purpose other than to subjugate the individual to the will of his examiner. This atmosphere carries its own badge of intimidation. To be sure, this is not physical intimidation, but it is equally destructive of human dignity. The current practice of incommunicado interrogation is at odds with one of our Nation's most cherished principles—that the individual may not be compelled to incriminate himself. Unless adequate protective devices are employed to dispel the compulsion inherent in custodial surroundings, no statement obtained from the defendant can truly be the product of his free choice.

. . .

*Together with No. 760, *Vignera v. New York,* on certiorari to the Court of Appeals of New York and No. 761, *Westover v. United States,* on certiorari to the United States Court of Appeals for the Ninth Circuit, both argued February 28—March 1, 1966; and No. 584, *California v. Stewart,* on certiorari to the Supreme Court of California, argued February 28—March 2, 1966.

To summarize, we hold that when an individual is taken into custody or otherwise deprived of his freedom by the authorities and is subjected to questioning, the privilege against self-incrimination is jeopardized. Procedural safeguards must be employed to protect the privilege, and unless other fully effective means are adopted to notify the person of his right of silence and to assure that the exercise of the right will be scrupulously honored, the following measures are required. He must be warned prior to any questioning that he has the right to remain silent, that anything he says can be used against him in a court of law, that he has the right to the presence of an attorney, and that if he cannot afford an attorney one will be appointed for him prior to any questioning if he so desires. Opportunity to exercise these rights must be afforded to him throughout the interrogation. After such warnings have been given, and such opportunity afforded him, the individual may knov ingly and intelligently waive these rights and agree to answer questions or make a statement. But unless and until such warnings and waiver are demonstrated by the prosecution at trial, no evidence obtained as a result of interrogation can be used against him.

IV.

A recurrent argument made in these cases is that society's need for interrogation outweighs the privilege. This argument is not unfamiliar to this Court. See, *e.g., Chambers* v. *Florida,* 309 U. S. 227, 240-241 (1940). The whole thrust of our foregoing discussion demonstrates that the Constitution has prescribed the rights of the individual when confronted with the power of government when it provided in the Fifth Amendment that an individual cannot be compelled to be a witness against himself. That right cannot be abridged. As Mr. Justice Brandeis once observed:

"Decency, security and liberty alike demand that government officials shall be subjected to the same rules of conduct that are commands to the citizen. In a gov-

117

ernment of laws, existence of the government will be imperilled if it fails to observe the law scrupulously. Our Government is the potent, the omnipresent teacher. For good or for ill, it teaches the whole people by its example. Crime is contagious. If the Government becomes a lawbreaker, it breeds contempt for law; it invites every man to become a law unto himself; it invites anarchy. To declare that in the administration of the criminal law the end justifies the means . . . would bring terrible retribution. Against that pernicious doctrine this Court should resolutely set its face." *Olmstead* v. *United States,* 277 U. S. 438, 485 (1928) (dissenting opinion).

In this connection, one of our country's distinguished jurists has pointed out: "The quality of a nation's civilization can be largely measured by the methods it uses in the enforcement of its criminal law."

If the individual desires to exercise his privilege, he has the right to do so. This is not for the authorities to decide. An attorney may advise his client not to talk to police until he has had an opportunity to investigate the case, or he may wish to be present with his client during any police questioning. In doing so an attorney is merely exercising the good professional judgment he has been taught. This is not cause for considering the attorney a menace to law enforcement. He is merely carrying out what he is sworn to do under his oath—to protect to the extent of his ability the rights of his client. In fulfilling this responsibility the attorney plays a vital role in the administration of criminal justice under our Constitution.

In announcing these principles, we are not unmindful of the burdens which law enforcement officials must bear, often under trying circumstances. We also fully recognize the obligation of all citizens to aid in enforcing the criminal laws. This Court, while protecting individual rights, has always given ample latitude to law enforcement agencies in the legitimate exercise of their duties. The limits we have placed on the interrogation process should not constitute an undue interference with a proper system of law enforcement. As we have noted, our decision does not in any way preclude police from carrying out their traditional investigatory functions. Although confessions may play an important role in some convictions, the cases before us present graphic examples of the overstatement of the "need" for confessions. In each case authorities conducted interrogations ranging up to five days in duration despite the presence, through standard investigating practices, of considerable evidence against each defendant. Further examples are chronicled in our prior cases. See, *e.g., Haynes* v. *Washington,* 373 U. S. 503, 518-519 (1963); *Rogers* v. *Richmond,* 365 U. S. 534, 541 (1961); *Malinski* v. *New York,* 324 U. S. 401, 402 (1945).

It is also urged that an unfettered right to detention for interrogation should be allowed because it will often redound to the benefit of the person questioned. When police inquiry determines that there is no reason to believe that the person has committed any crime, it is said, he will be released without need for further formal procedures. The person who has committed no offense, however, will be better able to clear himself after warnings with counsel present than without. It can be assumed that in such circumstances a lawyer would advise his client to talk freely to police in order to clear himself.

Custodial interrogation, by contrast, does not necessarily afford the innocent an opportunity to clear themselves. A serious consequence of the present practice of the interrogation alleged to be beneficial for the innocent is that many arrests "for investigation" subject large numbers of innocent persons to detention and interrogation. In one of the cases before us, No. 584, *California* v. *Stewart,* police held four persons, who were in the defendant's house at the time of the arrest, in jail for five days until defendant confessed. At that time they were finally released. Police stated that there was "no evidence to connect them with any crime." Available statistics on the extent of this practice where it is condoned indicate that these four are far from alone in being subjected to arrest, prolonged detention, and interrogation without the requisite probable cause.

Over the years the Federal Bureau of Investigation has compiled an exemplary record of effective law enforcement while advising any suspect or arrested person, at the outset of an interview, that he is not required to make a statement, that any statement may be used against him in court, that the individual may obtain the services of an attorney of his own choice and, more recently, that he has a right to free counsel if he is unable to pay. A letter received from the Solicitor General in response to a question from the Bench makes it clear that the present pattern of warnings and respect for the rights of the individual followed as a practice by the FBI is consistent with the procedure which we delineate today. It states:

"At the oral argument of the above cause, Mr. Justice Fortas asked whether I could provide certain information as to the practices followed by the Federal Bureau of Investigation. I have directed these questions to the attention of the Director of the Federal Bureau of Investigation and am submitting herewith a statement of the questions and of the answers which we have received.

" '(1) When an individual is interviewed by agents of the Bureau, what warning is given to him?

"The standard warning long given by Special Agents of the FBI to both suspects and persons under arrest is that the person has a right to say nothing and a right to counsel, and that any statement he does make may be used against him in court. Examples of this warning are to be found in the *Westover* case at 342 F. 2d 684 (1965), and *Jackson* v. *U.S.*, 337 F. 2d 136 (1964), cert. den. 380 U.S. 935.

" 'After passage of the Criminal Justice Act of 1964, which provides free counsel for Federal defendants unable to pay, we added to our instructions to Special Agents the requirements that any person who is under arrest for an offense under FBI jurisdiction, or whose arrest is contemplated following the interview, must also be advised of his right to free counsel if he is unable to pay, and the fact that such counsel will be assigned by the Judge. At the same time, we broadened the right to counsel warning to read counsel of his own choice, or anyone else with whom he might wish to speak.

" '(2) When is the warning given?

" 'The FBI warning is given to a suspect at the very outset of the interview, as shown in the *Westover* case, cited above. The warning may be given to a person arrested as soon as practicable after the arrest, as shown in the *Jackson* case, also cited above, and in *U. S.* v. *Konigsberg,* 336 F. 2d 844 (1964), cert. den. 379 U. S. 933, but in any event it must precede the interview with the person for a confession or admission of his own guilt.

" '(3) What is the Bureau's practice in the event that (a) the individual requests counsel and (b) counsel appears?

" 'When the person who has been warned of his right to counsel decides that he wishes to consult with counsel before making a statement, the interview is terminated at that point, *Shultz* v. *U. S.,* 351 F. 2d 287 (1965). It may be continued, however, as to all matters *other* than the person's own guilt or innocence. If he is indecisive in his request for counsel, there may be some question on whether he did or did not waive counsel. Situations of this kind must necessarily be left to the judgment of the interviewing Agent. For example, in *Hiram* v. *U. S.,* 354 F. 2d 4 (1965), the Agent's conclusion that the person arrested had waived his right to counsel was upheld by the courts.

" 'A person being interviewed and desiring to consult counsel by telephone must be permitted to do so, as shown in *Caldwell* v. *U. S.,* 351 F. 2d 459 (1965). When counsel appears in person, he is permitted to confer with his client in private.

" ' (4) What is the Bureau's practice if the individual

requests counsel, but cannot afford to retain an attorney?

" 'If any person being interviewed after warning of counsel decides that he wishes to consult with counsel before proceeding further the interview is terminated, as shown above. FBI Agents do not pass judgment on the ability of the person to pay for counsel. They do, however, advise those who have been arrested for an offense under FBI jurisdiction, or whose arrest is contemplated following the interview, of a right to free counsel *if* they are unable to pay, and the availability of such counsel from the Judge.' "

The practice of the FBI can readily be emulated by state and local enforcement agencies. The argument that the FBI deals with different crimes than are dealt with by state authorities does not mitigate the significance of the FBI experience.

The Miranda decision is also interesting for its discussion of the problems inherent in asserting the protection against self-incrimination under the Fifth Amendment as against the requirements of the authority to protect the public against crime. Chief Justice Warren's decision quotes from the Federal Bureau of Investigation which is presented as adhering to constitutional requirements in connection with their view in practice of the constitutional provision against self-incrimination.

Opinion of the Court.

III.

Today, then, there can be no doubt that the Fifth Amendment privilege is available outside of criminal court proceedings and serves to protect persons in all settings in which their freedom of action is curtailed from being compelled to incriminate themselves. We have concluded that without proper safeguards the process of in-custody interrogation of persons suspected or accused of crime contains inherently compelling pressures which work to undermine the individual's will to resist and to compel him to speak where he would not otherwise do so freely. In order to combat these pressures and to permit a full opportunity to exercise the privilege against self-incrimination, the accused must be adequately and effectively apprised of his rights and the exercise of those rights must be fully honored.

It is impossible for us to foresee the potential alternatives for protecting the privilege which might be devised by Congress or the States in the exercise of their creative rule-making capacities. Therefore we cannot say that the Constitution necessarily requires adherence to any particular solution for the inherent compulsions of the interrogation process as it is presently conducted. Our decision in no way creates a constitutional straitjacket which will handicap sound efforts at opinion, and Justices Stewart and Black dissented. (Footnotes are excluded.)